HIS WORD COMFORTS

VIMA DASAN, S.J.

HIS WORD COMFORTS

ST PAULS

Eight of the articles in this book were originally published in the *Catholic Gazette*.

Some of the Scripture quotations are taken from *The Jerusalem Bible,* published and copyright 1966, 1967, 1968 by Darton, Longman & Todd Ltd., and used by permission.

ST PAULS Publishing
187 Battersea Bridge Road, London SW11 3AS, UK
www.stpauls.ie

Copyright © ST PAULS 2002

ISBN 085439 643 8

Set by TuKan DTP, Fareham, UK
Printed by Interprint Ltd., Marsa, Malta

ST PAULS is an activity of the priests and brothers
of the Society of St Paul who proclaim the Gospel
through the media of social communication

CONTENTS

INTRODUCTION

Life is not a straight-line pattern. There is in our life's journey a fine pattern of lights and shadows; of hard and narrow places, intermingled with God's most extraordinary providences. God loves to interweave the golden threads of his love along the warp of our everyday experiences. If we shut out the thought of suffering in life, we end up with a false view of things. A minute to smile and an hour to weep in; a pint of joy to a peck of trouble; that is life. Therefore, it does no good for us to shun grief at any cost, but to be patient in its company and consider how best to live through it in peace. This little book concentrates on ten particular kinds of painful situations in life.

There are moments of intense **anxiety**, when we feel deep apprehension, concern and worry; when we simply feel unsure, threatened, or believe ourselves to be a failure. There are moments of acute **loneliness** and desolation, when we feel isolated like an island in the middle of an ocean, having no one to understand and support us. There are times when we are thrown into the pit of despair and in the iron clutches of depression, when we feel that things are going wrong in all directions. There are times, when at the loss of a beloved one in **death**, we feel like crying, 'My God, My God, why have you let this happen?' There are occasions when we are deeply wounded, hurt and frustrated, when the terrible fire of **anger** is about to consume our heart, when we are ready to hurl stones at anyone. There are periods when **sickness** prunes our body down which sheds its leaves like a tree; when it becomes like a broken vessel, emptied of ambitions and strivings. **Old age** is the only thing that comes to us without effort, whether we want it or not; we grow old when the illness that is to carry us off finally begins to strike from within and without. Along with our ability to do good, we all have a comparable capacity to do evil with the result that all of us often suffer from **guilt feelings**. There are those of us who suffer from **addictions** when we are at the mercy of powers that grip us at the point of crisis. Conjugal life is one of the great steps that most people take in life. While many marriages succeed, quite a few suffer **marriage break-up**. Like a flower, some marriages fade away leaving no trace, while others yield no fruits, and if they do, the fruit does not ripen.

In this book we do not discuss, argue or answer the question: Why so much pain and trials in human life? Nor did Jesus give any answer. His best treatment was forgiveness and kindness. There were occasions in Christ's life when doctors by the bedside of a sick man or a dead girl, discussed the human tribulations. Some specialists said the condition of the malady was hereditary, others said that the causes lay in the man's particular history. Jesus when pressed could give only this reply: This man became ill so that I could help him; this woman became lonely so God could be her friend. It is in this manner of Jesus that this book also deals with various grievous situations in human life.

Ordeals are more than nagging inconveniences, minor setbacks and disappointments, or mild hurts and frustrations. They are events of great magnitude which test us to the core. These events strike unpredictably, plunging us into chaos, exhausting our resources, turning our lives up-side-down and leaving us wondering whether we can possibly make it. Confronted with major losses, painful decisions and irreversible situations, we can either cling to life or become victims. At the same time, we can either do it all alone, or throw ourselves into God's merciful hands. This book counsels people in particularly painful conditions to do whatever they can by means of human remedies, but also encourages them to seek God's light and strength.

Whenever you are driving through the mountains in the late afternoon, you are surprised to find yourself in dark shadows when you know the sun is shining beyond your view. It is not a comfortable feeling; being in shadows at this time of the day does not seem right. But as you ascend the mountain, you are once again immersed in bright sunlight, only to begin the descent and re-enter the valley of shadows. The changing pattern of light and darkness in our lives is like this in many ways. Travelling through our valleys, we sometimes feel uncomfortable, and it takes a deeper act of faith to reassure ourselves that God is with us, though hidden from the view. When the light of God's grace falls on us afresh, we find new courage to go on. This is why every chapter in this book has a selection of God's word from the Scriptures. The word of God is not a pain-killer, but it can serve as a bright flame, or a guiding star, or a smooth path, or a kindly shepherd to the one who walks in the valley of darkness. God's word has grace in it, that heals our wounds, renews our strength, and pours dew on our dryness.

Therefore this little book *His Word Comforts,* is written with love, not so much to get one out of the pit, but to help him or her to find comfort. It is for those who find life a burden or a sentence to be got through, rather than a gift to be enjoyed. It is for those whose feelings of sorrow are greater than any feelings of joy. It is for those who mow the lawn and see not the green strips of our life's blessings, but the grass yet to be cut. This is a recipe book to be dipped into at a particular time of distress, with a hope to find some thought, or suggestion, or a word that may offer solace, support, encouragement, counselling, even a handy tip. Hence, it is both for those who walk on the ledge and for those pastors, counsellors, family and friends who help them to balance there.

Vima Dasan, s.j.

1

WHEN ANXIOUS

The official emotion of our age

John was my classmate in college, but a week before the finals he dropped out. He could not handle anxiety. During class tests he would break out in a cold sweat and his mind would go blank. He was in college for the first two years but later he stopped going to lectures; they were too scary for him, because he was afraid he would not be able to remember the important points that would come for the test. By the end of the second year, he felt uncomfortable even to enter the library. Soon he stopped going to the students' coffee bar, for he was afraid he would meet there some of his teachers or cleverer students. Then the amazing thing happened: he became almost too anxious to leave his living room. He is a Christian and so prays for peace, but still feels panic as he tries looking for a job. He wonders, "What if no one offers me a job?" "What if I get a job that I can't do?" "What if I get too anxious to go to work?"

Anxiety has been called "the official emotion of our age". If some are worried about the end of the world, others are worried about the end of the month! Blessed is the man who is too busy to worry in the day time and too sleepy to worry at night.

What is anxiety?

It is an intense feeling of apprehension, concern and worry. Anxiety can arise in response to some specific identifiable danger or in reaction to an imaginary or unknown threat. Normal anxiety comes to all of us at times, usually when there is some real danger. Neurotic anxiety is an exaggerated feeling of dread even when the threat is mild or non-existent. Moderate anxiety can be desirable and healthy because it helps us to avoid dangerous situations and leads to necessary action; but intense anxiety is more stressful for it interferes with our capacity to concentrate, causes forgetfulness, hinders efficiency in work, blocks effective relationships and can arouse panic.

Being aware

Anxiety can arise from various causes:
•   It can arise from threat. For example, I used to be afraid of the danger even in visiting my dentist. Most of us want to look good and do what we do well and hence we are threatened by anything that might harm our self-image. Separation could involve a threat. For example the death of a loved one, losing a partner through divorce or the break-up of an engagement can leave one feeling uncertain about the future. The undermining of values one cherishes, such as freedom, can also produce anxiety.
•   It can arise from conflict. A person may be faced with two options, both equally desirable, or both equally undesirable, or the one desirable and the other undesirable. For example, I may receive two dinner invitations on the same night, both will be

12

pleasant; you may be offered a new job with more money but which will cause the inconvenience of moving your household to a different area; a patient may be left to choose either to live with a painful illness or have a painful operation.

• It can arise from fear. Different people are afraid of different things. Some are afraid of failure, the future or nuclear war; others are afraid of rejection, intimacy or taking responsibility; still others are afraid of the futility and the meaninglessness of life; in some, anxiety arises because they have some irrational beliefs that create fear.

• It can arise from unmet needs. The basic human needs are survival, security, sex, being worthwhile, self-fulfilment and a sense of self-identity. If any of these needs is not met, a person is liable to become anxious.

• It can arise from physical disorders, leading a person to depression, hopelessness, feelings of guilt or even self-denial. If such an anxiety physically produced is properly diagnosed, medical treatment is often effective.

• There are still other sources of anxiety. If a person was taught as a child that being alone is dangerous, he feels anxious when nobody else is in the house. Some who are by nature more sensitive, hostile or insecure than others, become anxious more easily than others. Religious beliefs can either lead one to anxiety or offer deliverance from it. For example, if I believe in a God who is all-powerful and loving, I am less prone to anxiety than others who don't have such a belief.

Being on guard

• Guard against allowing your normal anxiety to turn into an intense, prolonged one. Such an uncontrolled anxiety can produce harmful physical reactions, such as ulcers, headaches, raised blood pressure and a variety of other stress diseases. It can also produce psychological reactions. For example, it can hinder our normal ability to think and remember, causing the mind to go blank at times. It can cause trouble in getting along with others or getting things done well.

• Guard against the defensive reactions so often seen in anxious people. Stop ignoring your feelings of anxiety and convincing yourself that there is nothing to worry about or blaming others for your own problem.

• Guard against turning away from God in times of worry. People, even religious ones, who are beset by worries tend not to find even a little time for prayer, for reading and reflecting on the Word of God or for attending church worship services. They become bitter against God for he seems to be silent in the face of crisis. Remember that God is most needed when we have worries.

HANDY TIPS

Relaxing: At regular intervals, do some relaxing exercises, such as: sit quietly, breathe deeply and try to relax the muscles. You can also tighten different groups of muscles, such as the fist or the shoulders, and then let the muscles relax as freely as possible. Sometimes it helps to close the eyes and imagine that you are relaxing on a beach or in some other calm surroundings. Such exercises may not remove the underlying causes of your anxiety but they will help you direct your attention away from your worries.

Keeping things in perspective: How we evaluate a situation depends very much on our perspective or point of view. Some people see the bad in everything; others are inclined to look at the bright side of life. Keep a realistic perspective that does not always lead you think that the worst is likely to happen.

Identifying the causes: Try to discover the sources of your anxiety. Ask yourself if any of those causes mentioned above may be creating your anxiety. Answer for yourself questions such as these: When am I most anxious? Do I get anxious when particular topics are discussed? What are the circumstances that have raised my present anxiety? When was the last time I felt really anxious?

Changing: If need be, try to change your lifestyle, relationships, place of residence or job, any of which could be causing anxiety.

Having a distraction: Involvement in some work and other activities will expend your nervous energy and serve as distraction away from your anxiety-producing situation.

Acting: Admit your anxiety, but plan a course of action to deal with it. You may use these three steps:

1. What is my problem? Write it down on a sheet of paper.
2. What should be done about this problem?
3. When, where and how should I begin? Plan a simple course of action.

Reaching out: If you care about others and reach out

to give help to those in need, you will find your own pressure lifted from your shoulders, giving you the energy to cope with your anxiety.

Seeking help: Seek help from someone who is a calm, supportive, and patient person. Such a person can also create in you self-confidence, a belief in your own abilities to meet the challenges and dangers of life. Such a caring support of a warm relationship can be a great help in times of anxiety.

HIS WORD COMFORTS

"I am telling you not to worry about your life and what you are to eat nor about your body and what you are to wear. Think of the flowers growing in the fields, they never have to work or spin; yet I assure you that not even Solomon in all his royal robes was clothed like one of these. Now if that is how God clothes the wild flowers which are there today and thrown into the furnace tomorrow, will he not much more look after you? So do not worry. Your heavenly Father knows you need them all." (Mt 6:25-32)

The basic cause of most of our worries is a failure to live our life on a day-to-day basis. The crosses which we make for ourselves by a restless anxiety as to the future are not crosses from God. Of course it is wise and prudent to plan for the future and to take responsible actions to solve our problems. The providence of God does not assist the idle and if I leap into a dry well foolishly, providence is not bound to fetch me out. But Jesus taught us that we should not be too anxious about the future or about life's basic needs, because we have a heavenly Father who knows what we need and will provide. A person who believes in what Jesus has said will agree with the hymn writer who wrote, "I know not what the future holds but I know who holds the future." In any case, it does not make sense to worry about the future: why open an umbrella before it starts to rain?

"We are well aware that God works with those who love him, those who have been called in accordance with his purpose and turns everything to their good." (Rom 8:28)

God is in control of all situations; he can mount the storm and walk upon the wind; when human plans are crossed and thwarted, God is able to turn every stumbling block into a stepping-stone. Those who believe in the sovereignty of God over their lives, will never get panic in any situation. When a train goes through a tunnel and gets dark, you don't throw away your ticket and jump off, you sit still and trust the engineer. Likewise when we are beset by worries, we must surrender all our needs to God and wait patiently, believing that he will lead us safely through our anxious moments. Hence, let our faith take up the cross, let our love bind it to our soul and let our patience bear it to the end.

"Come to me, all who are weary and burdened, and I will give you rest. Take my yoke upon you and learn from me, for I am gentle and humble in heart, and you will find rest for your souls. For my yoke is easy and my burden is light." (Mt 11:28-30)

When in despair, we work and work at change but nothing seems to happen. To work at it soon becomes a burden. Jesus asks us to come to him with our burden, for he will take it from us so that we can have rest. We must therefore resist the tendency to turn away from God in times of need, for left to ourselves, what can we do? He who trusts himself is lost, but he who trusts in God can do all things. Jesus is calling us to prayer in times of worries. Our prayer may be just a cry, but the best prayers have more often been groans than words. When we pray coincidences happen; when we do not, they don't. Hence, commit your persisting concerns in prayer to God who can not only release you from paralysing anxiety but also free you to deal realistically with the needs and welfare both of others and of yourself.

"Set your hearts on God's Kingdom first, and on God's saving justice, and all these other things will be given you as well." (Mt 6:33)

Everyone wants the Kingdom of God, but few want it first. Jesus asks us to seek God's Kingdom first. If we give God first priority in our lives, we can rest assured that our needs will be supplied and there will be no need to worry. What does it mean to seek God's Kingdom first? It means hungering and thirsting for God's favour, lest we be in perpetual hunger and thirst; it means endeavouring to live by faith: when we feel low and empty, it is not because the hand of God is tight-fisted but because the hand of our faith is weak; it means waging a ceaseless warfare against sin within us all the days of our life, for we know that Christianity is a battle and not a dream; it means taking a radical break to turn from earth's trash to heaven's treasure; it means labouring to have my bank in heaven rather than to have my heaven in a bank; it means holding loosely all that is not eternal.

A PRAYER

Dear God, I am empty, unsure, uncomfortable.
I feel threatened, and believe myself a failure.
The sea is so large and my boat is so small.
I anticipate the worst when time and time again,
the worst never happens.
To you alone, O Loving Father, I must cling,
running to your arms, there let me hide,
safe from all fears.
Lift me, O God, out of fear into hope;
out of frailty into strength;
out of foolishness into sense.
Calm my mind, help me to relax.
Let your comforting Spirit enter into me
and fill me with peace.

2

WHEN LONELY

Loneliness can be painful

I know a university professor well liked by his fellow professors and popular with his students as an excellent teacher. Some years ago he received his Ph.D. and he is presently doing post-doctoral research. To his credit, he has authored two books on economics. He is thus well settled with a successful career as both a scholar and teacher. But only people like me who are close to him know how intense is his feeling of loneliness, which he hides behind his lively personality and intellectual brilliance. He says that he does not have a single friend with whom he can talk about his personal problem. He is regularly in the midst of crowds but does not know any of them personally. After a busy day of teaching and research, he returns to his apartment, talks to his dog and gets lost reading a book. He does not go to any club to make friends, for he is afraid that no one would make the first move, especially if they find that he is a great scholar. Therefore, in spite of his professional achievements, he feels that he is a personal failure. He goes into depression quite often, for he has no one with whom he can relax and be himself. He recently told me that he might like to resign from his teaching job and move to some other place, but he is afraid that his loneliness would go with him. He complains that his loneliness is also interfering with his ability to concentrate.

What is loneliness?

Loneliness is not solitude. Solitude is voluntary isolation from others. One can willingly start and terminate solitude; it can be refreshing, revitalising and enjoyable. Solitude is not a mental problem with which people go seeking counselling. But loneliness comes when it is forced upon us against our own will. Loneliness can cling to us in spite of our best efforts to get rid of it; it is painful, draining and unpleasant. Loneliness is the problem with which many go to receive counselling.

Loneliness is primarily an inner feeling which one can experience even when surrounded by people. It comes when we see ourselves as isolated from others, or fail to find friends or lack the natural ability to relate to others. Very often people who are separated from God and hence find no meaning or purpose in their lives suffer from loneliness.

"Loneliness is the painful awareness that we lack close and meaningful contact with others. It involves a feeling of inner emptiness, isolation and intense longing. Even when they are surrounded by others, lonely people often feel left out, unwanted, rejected or misunderstood. There may be an intense desire to reach out but often the lonely person feels frustrated and unable to initiate, continue or experience a close relationship."

(Dr Gary R Collins)

But you are not alone

Remember that you are not the only one who is lonely. Loneliness, far from being a rare and curious phenomenon peculiar to yourself and few others, is now the central and inevitable fact of human existence. It has become one of the most universal sources of human suffering in the modern world. Some have called it the world's most common mental health problem. In many respects, ours is a lonely age. So many of us can apply to ourselves the words of Wordsworth: "I wandered lonely as a cloud that floats on high o'er vales and hills".

Millions of people, regardless of class or sex, suffer from loneliness, an inner emptiness that may flee after a few minutes or persist for a lifetime. There are children who are lonely because they are being bullied and dare not tell anyone; there are adults who are lonely because they find it hard to make friends; there are foreigners and refugees who are lonely because they feel rejected, isolated or discriminated against; there are spouses who are lonely because their partner has died or left them; and there are elderly people who are lonely because they miss their families and old friends. Yes, thousands of lonely hearts seek pitifully one prepared to accept them and so they go lonely side by side, but not together.

Being on guard

When we are lonely, we normally tend to look down upon ourselves as worthless, which is not true at all; because nobody wants me, to think I am good for nothing, is bad logic. Some lonely people, in their desperation and dejection, are moved by a strong but dangerous desire to seek any kind of relationship with any kind of people, which brings, in the end, only a pain more awful than loneliness itself. Many seek relief in bars, clubs or in encounter groups. While such attempts may bring some tentative and superficial relief, they would not really remove one's loneliness.

Guard against expressing your loneliness, as some do, through exhibitionist behaviour, such as wearing clownish clothing, just to attract people's attention; guard against falling into alcoholic and drug abuse as an escape from your loneliness. Beware! You might also try to express your lonely frustration in violent and destructive ways. Instead, do something about your loneliness before it becomes chronic or long lasting, causing even physical problems, such as heart disease or high blood pressure.

Keeping in mind

The causes of loneliness are varied. One has to keep them in mind to find a way out of loneliness.
• During times of changes and turmoil, many feel lonely. Rapid social changes in our modern world have created more lonely people than in the past, by isolating them from close relationship with each other. For example, technology has made people feel smaller and less needed. People are now more impersonal and shallow in their relationships. Modern transportation makes moving easier with the result that friendships are torn up, families are separated, neighbourhood is broken and community spirit at a very low ebb. Urbanisation has created a fear in cities

because of the prevalence of crime, leading city dwellers to suspicion and withdrawal. Television by its programme-content has promoted superficiality and aroused fear in the viewers, who have developed a habit of sitting in front of the screen seldom communicating with each other.

• Loneliness can sweep over us, if our basic human needs are denied. For example, every person needs to feel close bonds with other human beings and to feel accepted and wanted as he or she is. Therefore, when children feel unwanted, rejected or spurned by parents, spouses by their mates, pastors by their congregations or employees by their employers and co-workers, painful loneliness can creep in.

• People can suffer from life-long loneliness, if they are insensitive to the needs and personality traits of others, if they are accustomed to value things more than people and to judge a person's worth by outward appearance rather than by his or her quality as a person.

• There are still many more doors open, through which loneliness can enter into a person's life. For example, people with little self-confidence or those who don't know how to build smooth inter-personal relationships or those who can't take control of any given social situation, can easily succumb to loneliness. Those who become hostile and angry with others because of some real or imaginary injustice drive away others by their negative attitudes and constant complaining. There are also people who erect barriers to keep others out, through their fear of intimacy, fear of being rejected, fear of acting inappropriately in public or fear of being hurt.

• Some are lonely because of the special circumstances in which they find themselves. For example, foreigners or newcomers to an area, young people away from home for the first time, spouses recently divorced or widowed, older people who live alone and people with diseased or deformed bodies; all such people are especially prone to loneliness.

• Lastly but very importantly, loneliness can be caused by alienation from God through sin. In the beginning of creation, Adam and Eve enjoyed intimacy with God and with each other. But when they rebelled against God, they cut themselves off from God and began accusing one another. One could say that loneliness first started there. Our hearts are made for God and hence we become restless when we sin against him, alienating ourselves from God and from each other. Therefore one should ask: does my loneliness persist because I am ignoring God and refusing to confess my sins?

HANDY TIPS

The following suggestions are for dealing with your problem of loneliness effectively at its deepest level with a lasting solution.

Admitting: Admit that you are lonely, acknowledge that it is painful and decide to do something about it. Remember that when you admit that you are lonely, you are not admitting that you are a social misfit, for in our society, everyone is lonely at times.

Considering: Consider the specific causes that underlie your loneliness, for loneliness can arise from a variety of causes. It is easier and more effective to work on the sources of loneliness than on its symptoms.

Changing: Change your attitude to loneliness. Change your self-pity and pessimistic thinking about the unfairness of life. Even in the midst of disturbing and disheartening happenings around you, learn to see the bright side of things. Try to get involved in some daily occupations that bring you in touch with people, such as: work, play, creative hobbies, reading a daily newspaper, church attendance and meetings.

Developing: Develop self-esteem. Acknowledge your self-worth, your strengths and gifts, as well as your weaknesses. It is no use comparing yourself with people who are more popular and successful; by doing so, you will only become more convinced of your own inferiorities. Remember that in God's sight, every individual is valued and loved.

Reaching out: Take courage to reach out to others. What if people criticise or reject you? What if people don't respond to you? It is natural that you may be troubled by such questions. But remember that in life there is always some risk in everything we do; risk-taking is part of human growth. Try to find out what you have done or failed to do in the past to prevent people from getting close to you and correct them. Where there is will, there is a way. Counsellors can help you a good deal in this regard.

Learning: If you lack social and communication skills, you can learn them. Learn how to handle yourself in social situations, either with the help of books or some counsellors. Learn how to relate and effectively interact with others.

HIS WORD COMFORTS

"It is not good for man to be alone. I will make a helper suitable for him." (Gen 2:18)

God who created us knew that human beings need other human beings for happiness. So he created Eve and gave her to Adam saying: "Be fruitful and multiply and fill the earth." We can neither be alone nor lonely, if we live in fellowship with God and one another.

"It was the woman you put with me; she gave me some fruit from the tree and I ate." (Gen 3:12)

When Adam and Eve broke God's command not to eat the fruit of the forbidden tree, they sinned, with the result that not only was their communion with God broken but also their intimacy with each other fell apart and so they began accusing one another. Hence, when we restore our relationship with God through repentance for our sins, we are able to start a friendly relationship also with our neighbours.

"How great is the Lord our God! I waited patiently for the Lord's help; then he listened to me and heard my cry." (Ps 40:1)

God is powerful, sovereign and compassionate. He can change the course of events and circumstances if and when he wants. When surrounded by situations that seem to be unchangeable and defeating, one must remember that loneliness rarely lasts for ever, for God is in control of everything.

"For this is how God loved the world: he gave his only begotten Son, so that everyone who believes in him, may not perish but have eternal life." (Jn 3:16)

Loneliness resulting from one's own low self-esteem can be dealt with effectively by strong faith in God's love. People who convince themselves they are unattractive, incompetent or disliked by others, have only to believe that in God's sight every human being is valued and loved. The truth is that each of us has abilities and gifts that can be developed.

"Can anything cut us off from the love of Christ? I am certain of this: neither hardships or distress or persecution or death or life will be able to come between us and the love of God known to us in Christ Jesus our Lord." (Rom 8:35)

Human contact is not the only solution to loneliness. Loneliness never disappears completely until we come to Christ. He loves each of us with God's own love, unconditionally; he died for us; when we sin, he forgives us and welcomes us back to God. He wants to be our friend closer than a brother.

"How is it that you three were not able to keep watch with me even for one hour?" (Mt 26:40)

Jesus knows all our infirmities, including the feeling of loneliness. When he sweated blood in the Garden, crushed by anguish and fear, he was left alone even by his closest disciples. Hence if we go to him in our loneliness, he will offer comfort.

"He was there alone." (Mt 14:23)

To be lonely and to be alone are quite different. We can be lonely when we are not alone and we can be alone without feeling lonely. Jesus often went alone to pray in order to gain strength and give direction to his life. By prayer, he could restore a right relationship with God so that he could keep a right attitude towards himself and those around him. The same can happen to us when we are alone with God in prayer. He can inspire and enable us to reach out to others and relate to them and he can even make use of us as instruments to offer friendship to the lonely.

"Do you not realise that your body is the temple of the Holy Spirit who is in you and whom you received from God?" (1 Cor 6:19)

God's Holy Spirit lives inside every believer; he helps us, prays for us and makes us more Christlike. When we have no one to turn to, we can always commune with the Spirit who lives within us.

"For where two or three are gathered in my name, there am I in the midst of them." (Mt 18:20)

Much of life is group experience. We are beings who need group support. A group gives a chance for expression and experimental growth in thinking and feeling. We cannot live the life of a human being cut off from the social group. Therefore, neither can we live the life of a Christian apart from the Church which is the body of Christ here on earth. By baptism we were reborn into the church which has God for its centre. Therefore, belonging to and getting involved with the church is a sure way out of loneliness, for it not only provides us with a valid emotional support and a sense of moral values, but also meets the needs of our social nature at the highest possible level.

A PRAYER

Lord Jesus! I am lonely and desolate.
I feel isolated like an island in the middle of
*   an ocean.*
No one understands my feelings and I hesitate
to burden others with my troubles.
I have none to share my joys and sorrows.
By the loneliness of your suffering on the cross
penetrate me with your creative power.
Let your presence transform my loneliness
into fellowship with you and with others.
Enable me to unite this form of poverty
with all those who feel lonely.

3

WHEN DEPRESSED

A world-wide phenomenon

"I was young, I was male, I was going to be a doctor. Young men in the caring profession do not get depressed – or so I thought. In fact, I was on the edge of collapse. I had always had an up-and-down personality prone to flying moods that would come and go without reason. This time the blackness stayed with me. When a favourite patient died on me, I plunged into a pity of worthlessness. I was no good as a doctor, I had never achieved anything, I would always be a failure; I had difficulty getting off to sleep and woke early drenched in sweat. I lost all interest in sex and ate to stave off unhappiness. I went to the dean to tell him I was giving up medicine. I was ready to give up life itself. It was depression, of course, and I recognised it." (Michael Shooter)

This newspaper article is by a consultant in child and adolescent psychiatry with Gwent Community Health Trust. He goes on to say that one in five of us will become depressed at some point in our lives. At any one time, one in ten of us will be struggling with depression of some degree. Men are just as vulnerable as women, and may be even more so. Yes, depression is a world-wide phenomenon affecting people of all ages, though it appears to be increasing in teenagers and young adults. According to a recent report from the Royal College of Psychiatrists in London, depression in men may be as high as 65 per cent and suicide is three times more likely in men than in women. In the 16 to 24 age group of young single males, there has been a 75 per cent rise in suicide since 1982.

The 'common cold' of mental disorders

Depression is known as the 'common cold' of mental disorders and the most widespread psychiatric disease affecting mankind today. Though so common, it is a very complicated condition; it is difficult to define but can be somewhat described by its symptoms. In its milder form, depression may be a passing period of sadness following personal disappointment. But in its more severe form, it can overwhelm its victims with sadness accompanied by pessimism; apathy that makes it difficult to get oneself going; general fatigue along with loss of energy and an inability to take an interest in anything; low self-esteem often accompanied by self-criticism making one feel guilty, worthless and hopeless, and even suicidal. It may also include loss of spontaneity, insomnia and loss of appetite.

Where is it from?

- Depression often has a physical cause. Lack of sleep, insufficient exercise, the side effects of drugs, physical illness or improper diet can create it.
- Childhood experiences can lead to depression in

later life. Children who have been separated from their parents and raised in an institution deprived of continuing warm human contact show apathy, poor health and sadness which can develop into depression in later life.

• The experience of teenagers and adults in conflict with their parents, having trouble becoming independent, may increase the possibility of severe depression in later life.

• Stresses of life due to loss of an opportunity, a job, status, health, or possessions may stimulate depression.

• When we face situations over which we have no control, we get depressed, realising that our actions are futile no matter how hard we try.

• Negative thinking can produce depression. How we think often determines how we feel. If we think negatively, seeing only the dark side of life, then depression is inevitable.

• Depression can come from anger when it is held within and turned against oneself. Most anger begins from hurt. If the anger is not admitted and dealt with, it then leads to revenge. If revengeful action is not possible, one goes into depression.

• When a person feels that he or she has failed or done something wrong, guilt arises and along with it comes self-condemnation, frustration and other depressive symptoms.

Being aware

• Of myths: It is a myth, and not true: that depression always results from sin or a lack of faith in God; that depression is caused by self-pity; that it is wrong for a Christian ever to be depressed; and that depression can be removed permanently by spiritual exercises.

• Of realities of life: In our life, there are 'mountain-top days' when everything is going well. There are 'plain days' which are ordinary, when we are neither elated or depressed. There are 'valley days' when we trudge heavily through disappointments, and if they persist, they are days of deep depression.

• Of masked depression: In some people depression is hidden from themselves but it comes out in other ways such as physical symptoms, complaints, aggression, angry temper, heavy drinking, violence and self-destruction.

• Of other people's plight: People who have to live with a depressed person often feel burdened by his or her worrying, fatigue, and lack of interest in any social activities.

• Of remedies: There are effective treatments and cures for depression. Most of the treatments can reduce symptoms, at least with some people, and frequently depression can be eliminated completely.

• Of depression-prone situations: For example, a recent widow is expected to be depressed, especially on the first birthday, the Father's Day or the first anniversary of the death of her husband. For some of us, holidays such as Christmas can be depression-producing times if we are separated from our loved ones or have no money to buy presents.

• Of coping techniques: Surveys show that people who resist depression are those who have learnt to master and cope with the stresses of life. If you feel that you have some control over your circumstances, you are less likely to feel helpless and hence depressed.

• If your depression has a physical basis, seek a competent physician's help; change your eating habits if they are poor. Depression is sometimes best treated by changes in one's diet.

• If past influences or family pressures are creating the depression, discuss these problems with someone who could help you to see them in a different perspective and if possible to take remedial action.

• If the depression has resulted from stress that is due to some loss, acknowledge the loss, express the grief to someone and let it go.

• If you are depressed due to a habit of negative thinking about yourself, re-evaluate your self-critical thoughts. Because of some disappointments, are you saying, "This proves I'm no good", or "I never do any-thing right", or "Nobody wants me now"? Remember, such self-criticisms are often not based on solid facts.

• If you lack energy or motivation to do something worthwhile try to get involved first in daily routines and activities in which you are likely to succeed.

• If your environment is causing depression, try to modify routines, reduce work loads or take periodic vacations.

• If you are depressed because you are lonely and isolated, join church or other social groups where you feel welcome and accepted. Reach out to others to serve them. Those who reach out to help others are the ones who benefit and are helped most.

HIS WORD COMFORTS

"Jesus Christ is the reflection of God's glory and bears the impress of God's own being, sustaining all things by his powerful command." (Heb 1:3)

When you are depressed because you face situations which are beyond your control, first see whether you can control at least a portion of your environment. Secondly, acknowledge the inevitability of some uncontrollable events in your life. As a bird can roost only on one branch and a mouse can drink no more than its fill from a river, so man can control only those events which man can. As the acceptance of what is possible is the beginning of happiness, so the acceptance of what is impossible is the beginning of wisdom. Thirdly, believe that everything is under the control of God who is the power that holds even the sky's majesty. Even the devil is God's devil. God has always the last word. God is so powerful that he can direct any evil to a good end. To our limited mind, the way of God is complex and hence hard for us to predict, but when God moves the pieces, they somehow come into a kind of order. With God there are mysteries, but no mistakes.

"Let your minds be filled with everything that is true, everything that is honourable, everything that is upright and pure, everything that we love and admire."
(Phil 4:8)

Each of us talks silently to ourselves. If this self-talk is nearly always negative, that can lead one into depression. If you are in the habit of saying to yourself, "I am worthless," recall what the Bible says: "As you think in your heart, so you are." Be a friend to yourself and others will be so too. Respect yourself if you want others to respect you. You are worth your own estimation of yourself. If you can look in the mirror and smile at what you see, then there is hope for you. If you are in the habit of seeing only the bad in people and in the world, recall what Shakespeare said: "There is nothing either good or bad but thinking makes it so."

Remember that there is a lot of good in the world. The sky is not less blue because the blind man does not see it.

Be an optimist. An optimist says his glass is half-full, while the pessimist says his glass is half-empty. Meditate on the Word of God, on things which are positive, good and just. Meditation is a form of self-talk that directs our minds away from negative thinking that leads to depression.

"Then Peter went up to him and said, 'Lord, how often must I forgive my brother if he wrongs me? As often as seven times?' Jesus answered, 'Not seven, I tell you, but seventy seven times.'" (Mt 18:21)

When we are hurt we get angry and anger hides the hurt; when we are angry we want to take revenge and revenge hides the hurt and anger; when we are revengeful, we want to take a destructive action; but if that is not possible, we go into depression. A Christian solution to this kind of depression is forgiveness. Forgive from your heart the one who has hurt you. Jesus asks us to forgive repeatedly. Forgive and then forget what you have forgiven. How easily we forget kindnesses, but store up injuries for ever in the back of our heads as if they are ancient relics! It is better to forget and smile than to remember and be sad. If you go down the path of unforgiveness, at the end of it you will find no stream but only a desert with twisted roots of bitterness pushing you to take revenge; and revenge never repairs an injury; how can blood be washed with blood? It is more honourable, therefore, to bury an injury than to revenge it.

"For to be sorrowful in a way that God approves leads to repentance and then to salvation with no regrets; it is the worldly kind of sorrow that ends in death." (2 Cor 7:10)

One may realise that his or her depression is due to guilt feeling accompanied by self-condemnation for having done something wrong. Of course, sin brings with it inner suffering to a guilty conscience. As virtue is its own reward, so vice is its own punishment. You cannot do wrong without suffering wrong. But there is the God of mercy who forgives all our sins. Our God is a big eraser; when he pardons, he consigns the offence to everlasting forgetfulness. Hence, go to him with a repentant heart, and reveal your sore wound and beg for his healing. He will send forth his healing Spirit into the dark places of your guilt. But take care that your repentance is not a worldly sorrow which is just remorse; remorse is impotent for it will sin again and will end in death. Have therefore a Godly sorrow which is constructive and brings repentance that leads to salvation and leaves no regret.

"I have learnt to manage with whatever I have; to live in prosperity or poverty. There is nothing I can't do in the One who strengthens me. And my God will fulfil all your needs out of the riches of his glory in Christ Jesus."
(Phil 4:12-18)

Sometimes we are plunged into depression because we have to face disappointments or have lost something valuable or have been rejected or failed in some important enterprise. Such periods of unhappiness and discouragement come to everyone. Even so, there are some ways by which we can prevent or soften the blows of depression. One sure way is trust in God. If God is God, he is perfect, lacking nothing that we need. If God is God then no insoluble problem exists and if God is your God then no problem of yours is without a solution. God is closer than our breathing and nearer than our hands and feet, especially when we are in difficulty. It is true that we can't always trace God's hand but we can always trust his heart for his love is equal to his greatness. God loves us because we are loveable, yes, but more so because he is love. Learn to see your circumstances through God's love instead of seeing God's love through your circumstances.

"I have told you all this so that you may find peace in me. In the world you will have hardships, but be coura-geous: I have conquered the world." (Jn 16:33)

Those who expect trials as part of life, including Christian life, will remain always prepared to face them and thus save themselves from falling too easily into depression. Perpetual sunshine is not usual in this world, neither it is good for us. There is no getting through this world without being scratched. Trials are certainly not intended for our pleasure but they are for our profit. Trials offer us occasion to demonstrate our character. We come out wiser through adversity. Jesus died in order to take away the curse from us, yet not to take away the cross from us. Jesus promised heaven after death, not before it.

But our trials strengthen our spiritual muscles; our afflictions prepare us for receiving the grace of God. In the darkness of our miseries, the grace of God shines more brightly. That is why Christian people are at their best, paradoxically, when they are in the furnace of affliction.

A PRAYER

Lord Jesus Christ!
I am in despair and in the iron clutches of
    depression.
Things are going wrong in all directions.
I feel the heart of my soul is tearing into two;
I need you to come and live there yourself.
Darkness is pressing all around me;
I can't fight this darkness by beating it with
    my hands.
I am still yours, Lord;
from the depth of my heart I call on you;
my soul waits for you, for in your word is all
    my trust.

I hold up my weakness to your strength;
my confusion to your compassion;
my affliction to your great agony on the cross.
May the depression I am feeling be for healing;
anoint the wounds of my spirit with the balm
    of forgiveness;
pour the oil of your calm on the waters of my
    heart.
Turn my face gently towards you;
keep my heart loving,
and my will determined to fight on to the end.

4

WHEN GRIEVING

Whenever a part of life is lost or taken away, it brings grief. What we lose could be a spouse by divorce or a leg by amputation or a car by selling. At any such loss, we experience deprivation and sadness. But a loss of a loved one by death can be devastating, for it lands us in an irreversible situation that no human power can change. We can never make death beautiful by dressing up the corpse in silk or surrounding it with flowers. Nothing throws us off balance like the death of someone important to us. When my father died, I felt as if my whole self had been thrown up into the air and was floating down in little pieces; I never knew how the little pieces would come together. It is possible to provide security against other ills, but as far as death is concerned, we all live in a city without walls. Death is never sweet, not even when it is suffered for the highest ideals.

Being aware

It is as natural to die as to be born. Everything on earth fades fast and death will take us all at last. You cannot take up a newspaper without finding that death has a corner in it. Death is more universal than life in this: that everyone dies but not everyone lives.

None of us know when we shall die but all of us know we must die. However, for life to continue, we all need loss and death. Loss and growth are partners in life. The caterpillar that goes into the darkness and silence of the cocoon must stop being a caterpillar, in order to become a brilliant butterfly. That is why people who have come through intense grief over the loss of their dear one often feel that they have had a painful but refining experience, with new strength to pick up a thread and draw in a string and then a rope leading back to a fuller life.

Being on guard

Guard against refusing to acknowledge the loss, to express your grief openly and to let it go. If you refuse, your otherwise normal and healthy grief may turn into a pathological and abnormal grief. If you refuse to acknowledge the loss for what it is, you will be unwilling to talk about the deceased, persist in deep depression, withdraw from society and even indulge in subtle threats of self-destruction. If you refuse to express your grief, you are holding back on it. As a result, you will react to anything with anger, look for someone or something to blame for the loss, feel guilty as if you were responsible for the loss, and thus prevent your own healing. In fact, if you drown your sorrowful emotions that are straining to be released, they will not disappear; rather, your grief will show itself again at a later time, when you may have to face other losses, even insignificant ones. If you refuse to let it go, you keep yourself in bondage to the deceased person and deny yourself freedom to move on with life.

Admit the loss: Acknowledge it willingly and openly. Until you acknowledge it, you will not be able to grieve it. Do not ignore the pain of the loss but get in touch with it and bring it to the surface.

Manifest your grief: Healthy and meaningful expression of our emotions facilitate our passage through the grief-tunnel. Emotions are God-given gifts. Befriend them and express them in an appropriate way. Talk with someone about your relationship with the deceased and how the loss is affecting you and your life. If you are on the verge of tears, shed them. To weep is to make less the depth of grief. They that sow in tears shall reap in joy. You may like to go to some grieving rituals such as a wake, funeral or memorial service, which offer help to make death more real and serve as safety-valves for the heart with too much pressure upon it.

Let it go: Choose to change things that keep you tied to the person or object lost. For example, if you have lost your child, choose to give some of the child's belongings to needy children. Choose to make use of the room where the deceased stayed for some new purposes, and do not keep it locked indefinitely. Keep some of the belongings of the deceased yourself and give the rest away to people who could use them. Let it go.

HIS WORD COMFORTS

"Jesus saw her weeping; his heart was touched and he was deeply moved." (Jn 11:32)

Jesus knows that it is sweet to mingle tears with tears; so you are not alone weeping. When Lazarus died and Jesus saw his sisters' tears, he too wept, because he was aware of the pain of those close to Lazarus. Do you know that Jesus weeps with you? How can Jesus, who taught us to feel another's woe, remain unmoved when we grieve?

And concerning the resurrection of the dead, have you not read what was said to you by God, "I am the God of Abraham, the God of Isaac, and the God of Jacob"? God is not the God of the dead but of the living.
(Mt 22:31-32)

"I have come so that they may have life and have it to the full." (Jn 10:10)

If so, why should God allow us to suffer and die? Well, that is going to remain a mystery to the end of time. When Job asked about it, God did not answer, but he simply asked Job: "Where were you when I laid the earth's foundations?" (Job 38:4). However, we are able to have some understanding into the mystery of suffering. Human sorrow shatters the illusion of human self-sufficiency, breaking through the deception that we are in control of our life. Through sorrow we are able to sense who we are and why we must reach beyond ourselves to God. To be somewhat parched by the heat and drenched by the rain of life do refine the human spirit, for every pain we welcome destroys something of wickedness in us. Above all, we believe that fuller life that Jesus came to give us depends on how more fully we carry out God's will; and God's will is that we love him and our neighbour. Is not love essentially sacrificial? Yes it is; the presence of pain tells us how great love is, and a love that rejects any suffering soon begins to sicken and decay.

"Unless a wheat grain falls into the earth and dies, it remains only a single grain; but if it dies, it yields a rich harvest." (Jn 12:24)

God does not take pleasure in seeing us suffering, as we may take pleasure in gazing at the waves of the sea disturbed by the winds. However, in order to have life, every seed must burst apart and let go of what it is; for the fruit to appear, it must pass from the view and die away; it must sink its roots down into the earth's dark bosom, in order to push its stem up towards the sun. It happened to Jesus. He died, but not only did he rise to glory but his life lives in us too.

"We shall not all die, we shall all be changed, the dead will be raised never to die again. Our perishable nature must put on imperishability, our mortal nature must put on immortality. Thanks be to God who gives us the victory through our Lord Jesus Christ."
(1 Cor 15:52-56)

We Christians believe that through his death and resurrection, Jesus has given us eternal life. His death is our life, his loss is our gain. Christianity is the most monumental fraud, if there be no eternal life. Why, then, cling on to grief over a Christian's death? Grief over what? Over the spirit's glad release, to pass from pain to perfect peace?

"Death where is thy sting? Death where is thy victory?"
(1 Cor 15:54)

45

This is the boldest and bravest challenge that man ever sent ringing in the ears of death. Death is here out-braved, called a coward and bidden to do his worst. Human spirit never dies and death can never kill what never dies. If our birth makes us mortal, our death makes us immortal.

"If anyone wants to be a follower of mine, let him renounce himself and take up his cross and follow me."
(Lk 9:23)

A crossless Christ cannot be our Saviour as a Christless cross cannot be our refuge. So, Jesus carried his cross and asks us to carry ours. Hence, willingly take up your cross which is right now the loss you grieve. Do not ignore it but look at it and grieve over it and let it go. Do not look elsewhere for your holiness; it is right here in your loss, for it was on the cross Jesus won our salvation. If you accept this cross, the pain of it will become less and less, because the chief pang of most losses is not so much the actual suffering itself, as our own spirit of resistance. If you accept it and carry it, you may feel that your heart is cast in the cruel fire of sorrow; but then you will soon realise that your heart has been refined and you will only bless the cleansing fire. Offer your grief to Jesus on the cross, where all the sorrow in the world was gathered together into his one redemptive sorrow.

A PRAYER

My God, my God, why have you let this happen? You create us, but why uncreate?

You are the source of love; but why rip away
the one I so loved?
As I cry to you from the pit of darkness,
to reach out to the one I loved but can't touch,
hold me and stay with me.
Your Son Jesus Christ by dying has
destroyed death,
by rising has restored our life.
Dispel therefore the shadow of death,
with the bright dawn of life.
Lift me from the depth of grief,
into the peace and light of your presence.
Comfort me and embrace me with your love.
Give me hope in my confusion,
and grace to let go the loss into a new life.

5

WHEN ANGRY

It is good

Frank was in a hurry but the kids were dawdling. He was in the car with the engine running and he was already a bit late and felt that his family didn't seem to appreciate this. Calmly telling them to move along would have fallen on deaf ears. So he yelled, "Hurry up you kids, or I'll go to the film alone. I hate to be kept waiting." His growl made the kids move in ways they wouldn't normally if they did not think the issue was urgent. Frank showed his anger deliberately with inner calm while looking like a tiger on the outside. Anger is one of the God-given emotions and hence is good, useful and necessary. The Scriptures often speak of God getting angry. But God's wrath is directed towards sin and sinners. God's anger is never capricious or self-indulgent. It is vigorous and intense, yet is always controlled and consistent with his love and mercy. Jesus too was angry. He became so angry with money changers in the Temple that he made a whip out of cord and drove them away. But his anger was at the disrespect for God's house, at the hypocrisy and pride of the Pharisees. So too, our anger is good if it is directed at changing a behaviour from bad to good, or at establishing truth and justice, or in physical self-defence. Our anger is good if it does not arise from hostility but tries to set things right in a non-violent way if possible. It is good if it means being firm and assertive but not hostile. It is good even when you are furious outside, but forgiving and understanding inside.

Anger is bad

• If it gets you in trouble, eats your guts out and makes a complaining, whining baby out of you.
• If it increases your frustration. The wife who resents her husband's coming home late for dinner, and who gives him a piece of her mind, may make matters infinitely worse by accusing him of being unfaithful.
• If it prevents you from solving problems. Anger is not a solution to frustration but only a reaction to it. Yelling at your daughter for cramming the washing machine does not show her how to wash clothes properly.
• If it leads to child abuse. Some parents lose patience because a baby cries all night. When they strike out at the child they are fully aware of their frustration. What will that child be like when he is grown up and has children of his own, if he is beaten daily now?
• If it results from jealousy. A jealous person is a fear-filled person with a very severe case of inferiority, which he tries to overcome almost exclusively by the reactions others have to him. If his loved ones pay him plenty of attention, he is fine, but if they pay attention to others, he panics.
• If it covers up fear. Angry people often cover up deep fears of inadequacy and failure. Some parents can't stand being corrected. Should a child show where mum or dad is mistaken, the parent becomes

defensive and angry because his or her authority is questioned.
• If it arises from self-pity. The self-pitier is his own enemy. When I pity myself, I first have to make a mountain out of a molehill, thus making catastrophes out of annoyances.

Anger is wrong

• When it is the source of bitterness, hatred, revenge and an attitude of judgement.
• When it turns into aggressive and destructive behaviour, inflicting on others pain or pressure: either directly, by lashing out verbally, physically, psychologically or socially; or indirectly, by directing the anger not on the source of it but on some other innocent; or passively, as in gossiping and spreading damaging stories.
• Instead of using my anger to lead another person to repent and change for the better, when I pretend to be concerned about the other person's good while actually using it as an excuse for expressing my own hostility.
• Christians are called to express anger if charity demands. Hence it is wrong to deny, ignore, distort or refuse to share our true feelings in a way that lets others know that we feel hurt.

The sequence of getting angry

Step One: "I want something" – We all have millions of desires. Our wants are literally as vast as our imagination.

Step Two: "I didn't get what I wanted and am frustrated" – We can't get all that we want in this world; it is one of the unavoidable regrets we must live with.

Step Three: "It is awful and terrible not to get what I want" – Is it so? Should we always have our own way? Is being frustrated always unbearable?

Step Four: "You shouldn't frustrate me! I must have my way" – I wanted something which was merely a healthy wish, but now I have turned it into a demand and think that if I don't get it, the sky will fall.

Step Five: "You are bad for frustrating me" – Until now, I have only been angry, not hateful and vengeful, but now I have judged someone bad and evil because he or she frustrated me.

Step Six: "Bad people ought to be punished" – Not because it will necessarily do him some good but because he is not good enough to deserve anything but pain and blame.

Being aware

• Anger is infectious. Should a husband scold the waiter for poor service, his wife is also likely to feel indignant.

• Anger if suppressed for a long time can cause physical ills such as high blood pressure. It can strain a weak heart to a dangerous point.

• Many divorces have their root in anger. It is not things like money, sex, in-laws, jobs, or coming home late, but getting angry over these frustrations.

• Anger comes from your thinking, not from the things you are thinking about. First get hold of yourself emotionally and then you can do something about your frustration.

- Annoyance is not catastrophe. We often blow situations up out of all proportion and then we get scared of the monsters we have created.
- Frustrations are not disturbances. Frustration is the condition of wanting something and not getting it but disturbance is my anger over not getting what I want.
- It is what you do about a frustration that counts, not how much you shout about it. If complaining works, well and good. But too often it does not and then action is needed.
- Blame is at the heart of anger. Blame means condemning someone, which is not justified. Instead of blaming people for their actions, it is wiser to separate their behaviour from themselves.
- To force anger out of awareness and deny I am angry, can be unhealthy. It may give a temporary relief but in time, pressure builds until it bursts.
- A single event can make one person livid with anger, but hardly seems to bother someone else. Partly, this difference depends on personality differences or on the ways in which a situation is perceived.

HANDY TIPS

Admit anger: Anger that is denied will never be eliminated. Such an admission may be threatening, but realise that it is a God-given emotion and hence one need not be ashamed of it.

Express anger: To express is not to vent hostility by letting off steam, swearing and screaming. Instead use harmless ways such as sports and hobbies to redirect your energy. Try to deal with your hurts one at a time. Tell the other person why it has hurt and made you feel angry.

Consider the sources of anger: Ask yourself: What is making me angry? Am I jumping to conclusions about the person or situation making me angry? Is there something threatening to make me feel afraid or inferior? Am I angry because my expectation is unrealistic? Is there anything I can do to change the situation to feel less angry?

Avoid anger-producing situations: Sometimes duty or wisdom requires that we face frustrating situations. Even so, there are times when we can stay away from them.

Re-evaluate situations: The best athletes remain calm and unangered even when they are provoked by opposition players, because, in preparing mentally for the game, they have learnt to expect setbacks and have rehearsed ways to handle them.

Increase your self-esteem: Anger is less destructive and more easily controlled when you are secure as an individual and not plagued by inferiority or self-doubt.

Avoid brooding: When feeling angry, do not go on ruminating on the causes of anger which will only build up in you a negative and bitter mind-set. Replace it with positive and less critical thinking.

Learn to confront: You can learn to tell another person how you feel, what you think or want, not in a manner of critical confrontation that stimulates anger but gently and in love.

HIS WORD COMFORTS

"Let all bitterness and anger and clamour and evil speaking be put away from you with all malice."

(Eph 4:31)

When we are hurt, we become bitter and bitterness leads to angry emotional expressions, exploding in far-reaching and disruptive actions, wrecking the lives of persons, homes, communities and even nations. If you are bitter at heart, sugar in the mouth will not help you. What will help is striking at the root of bitterness, and the root is malice. Malice is bad intent and desire to harm. Malicious people desire the unhappiness of others more than their own happiness. They like others much better when they are battered down by a siege of misfortunes than when they triumph. As a kid I was told by a teacher that I should never trust a malicious man for he is like a serpent that will still bite though it may have been kept tamed a long time. Therefore, in the place of malice and bitterness, we must develop goodwill and under-standing towards others. Goodwill is kindness in action and goodness is the only investment that will never fail. Understanding is seeing through others as we see through ourselves. The way to health and peaceful living can be found only when we move towards goodwill and understanding and a view of life that has the motto: "Malice towards none and charity for all".

"Let every man be swift to hear, slow to speak and slow to human anger, for the anger of man never serves the righteousness of God." (Jas 1:19-20)

We so easily ascribe to our angry impulse the dignity of God's own righteous indignation. Since God is perfect, omniscient and always accurate in seeing things, his anger is always just against some form of evil. But we as human beings are imperfect and see each situation from our own point of view and are liable to make wrong judgements. Hence our anger need not always be righteous indignation. We are therefore advised to curtail our tendency to judge people as soon as we are hurt. How easily we judge ourselves by our best intentions but others by their worst faults! Judging others is like measuring another's coat on my own body. How foolish! One way not to allow our anger to grow intense is to guard our words. In anger some people speak positively awful, others awfully positive, still others unprintable, words. Words can make a deeper scar than silence can ever heal, The tongue has no bones but it can break your back. Be sparing and slow when you speak, but listen more while trapped in an angry conversation. The reason why we have two ears and only one mouth is that we may listen the more and talk the less.

"If we acknowledge our sins, he is trustworthy and upright, so that he will forgive our sins and will cleanse us from all evil." (1 Jn 1:9)

To admit that we are angry and acted aggressively can be a humbling experience; but we need to be humble. Humility and sanity go together as pride and madness do. To be humble is to be truthful in acknowledging one's faults. As we must have self-esteem, so we must have self-knowledge that we are weak humans. Only an egoist thinks he has no faults; he is an 'I' specialist whose self-importance makes his mind shrink while his head swells. If in all humility we acknowledge before God our uncontrolled anger and acts of aggression, he will forgive us and heal us. When God forgives, what is broken is made whole, what is soiled is made clean. How many times in the past have we gone to God as our last resort and learnt that the

55

storms of life had driven us not upon the rocks but into a bed of blessings!

"Yes, if you forgive others their failings, your heavenly Father will forgive you yours. But if you do not forgive others, your Father will not forgive your failings either."
(Mt 6:14-15)

If we do not forgive those who have hurt us, our anger along with any accompanying sinful side-effects will not be forgiven. This means that if we hold grudges, our anger is certain to continue with all the accompanying misery and tension. Hence we must forgive. A Christian can always afford to forgive and can never afford not to. We must forgive others, lest we break the bridge over which we must pass ourselves, for everyone is in need of forgiveness. Besides, as St Augustine said, "If you are suffering from a bad man's injustice, forgive him, lest there be two bad men." When we forgive we are less bogged down by anger and thus better able to focus our energies on more healthy activities.

"The fruit of the Spirit is love, joy, peace, patience, kindness, trustfulness, gentleness and self-control."
(Gal 5:23)

When we get angry, reason often gives way to feeling, which in turn, if not controlled, leads us to say something rash or do something aggressive, which might be regretted later. Therefore we need to cultivate self-control. If I want to be superior to external influences, I must first become superior to my passions. There is a raging tiger inside every one of us. The sooner we build inside ourselves a cage to pen that tiger in, the better. We can gain self-control through the help of the Holy Spirit. One might as well try to catch sunbeams with a fish hook as to try to have self-control unassisted by the Holy Spirit. Hence we must grow spiritually, led by the Spirit. Spirit-filled life is not a special deluxe edition of Christianity; it is the growing experience of hunger and thirst after right-eousness. Once we have learnt to live in the Spirit, we will observe a slow decline in anger, strife and other deeds of the flesh and we will also notice an increase in love, patience, gentleness, self-control and other fruits of the Spirit. We could not attempt to raise flowers if there were no atmosphere, or produce fruits if there were no light or heat. So too, we cannot experience the fruits of the Spirit without the Holy Spirit.

A PRAYER

Here I am, O Lord, wounded, hurt and
   frustrated.
The terrible fire of anger is about to consume
   my heart.
I am ready to let rip, to hurl a stone at anyone
   in front;
to pound my fists into a brick wall and lash out;
to shout and rip sheets into shreds and curse.
Lord, pick me up and put me together again;
calm the waves of this heart, calm its tempests;
take away this cup of bitterness,
break my anger though my heart has been
   broken;
through the storms of fury, guide me to the shore.

I do not so much ask you to prevent the storms,
as to keep me firm within them.
I am prone to blame others for every wrong;
take from my eyes the dust that blinds me,
that I may treat others by the light of your
*   compassion;*
your compassion can restore my brokenness.
Give me the true courage that shows itself by
*   gentleness;*
give me the true wisdom that shows itself by
*   patience;*
give me the true power that shows itself by
*   self-control.*

6

WHEN SICK

Angela Brown was 70 years old. During her whole life, except for occasional colds and flu, she had been in reasonably good health. She had almost never gone to a doctor with any serious complaint. But the crisis came suddenly. On that fateful October afternoon, her entire life turned upside down. After lunch, she found herself gasping for breath. She wanted to lie down but could not raise herself from her chair. "This must be the end," her husband heard her muttering. Within minutes, the paramedics came and began to administer oxygen. By the time she got to the hospital, she was feeling better. The doctor ordered a batch of tests and that made Angela very anxious. Two weeks later, when she faced the doctor, her usual self-composure disappeared. "Angela, it looks like you have the beginning of lung cancer," said the doctor. She could not believe what she heard. Over the following weeks, she saw several specialists, hoping that someone would tell her it was not true. But all confirmed the diagnosis. After few weeks in the hospital, she came home. But for the next several months, her life seemed to revolve around medicines and hospitals. Her kidneys began to fail, her strength and energy waned and she began to develop bed sores. She increasingly struggled with sleeplessness and stomach upsets because of medications, but she kept her sense of humour and rarely uttered a word of complaint during her long illness. One evening, the doctor, who sat near her bed, told her the truth: "Angela, we have done all that we could, but I want to be honest; you are not going to get any better; all that remains for us to do is to make you feel as comfortable as we can." One December morning, after fifteen months of battle against illness, Angela died peacefully in her sleep.

"We are fearfully and wonderfully made"

Our body is amazing. We stand in awe before the complexity of our body and the Creator who made it. Yet the human body sheds its leaves like a tree, when sickness prunes it down. Diseases attenuate our bodies, dry them, wither them and shrivel them like old apples. Sickness not only batters our body but it can also crucify its soul. Whenever I am ill, I feel that my very goodness is sickly. When we do not understand what is wrong with our body and when we don't know when or if we will get better, we become anxious, worried and afraid. What is worse is that sickness comes on horseback and departs on foot. If the sickness persists, we start asking the usual but unanswerable question, "Why me?" Illness, together with the loss of a sense of well-being, brings with it other losses too, such as the loss of a part of the body, or one's job or independence or self-esteem. How much we wish that we had always a sane mind in a sound body! After all, what is life, if it is just living but not living in health? However, we can't deny that sickness has also a bright side to it.

The bright side

• Physical illness shatters our irrational belief that we are self-sufficient and are masters of our own destiny. When we are sick we are forced to comply with doctor's orders. We are told what and when medicine is to be taken. We are expected to submit to a variety of diagnosis and treatment.

• Illness strikes a blow at our unhealthy human tendency to avoid people, especially strangers so that we can live our life undisturbed by others. When we are sick, we are often forced to put our lives and our bodies into the hands of strangers with whom we may have no close personal ties.

• Physical illness helps us to slow down and gives us a breathing space to get hold of our life, if not physically, at least emotionally and spiritually.

• Physical illness brings us face to face with our limitation, gives us a clearer picture of human life on earth and turns our minds to eternity. In health we forget ourselves and our destinies but temporary sickness reminds us of these concerns.

• Illness provides a great opportunity to be alone with God, for the simple reason that the sick have plenty of time to themselves free from other activities. Being alone with God in prayer can lead the sick to wholeness of spirit, even if wholeness of body is never possible.

Being aware

• People show differences in their tolerance of pain. Some people feel little pain even with a major illness, but others feel great pain even without a discernible organic disease. Many of these individual differences result, unless there is a biological cause, from a person's attitudes to pain, and family background or personal values and religious beliefs.

• Sick people who become easily depressed and frustrated because they feel so helpless, do not actually help themselves. Such a negative attitude only slows down recovery. In contrast, those sick persons who cheerfully accept their sickness and try to make the best of their physical problems, often feel better and recover faster.

• Surveys have shown that those heart attack victims who constantly grumble about their illness and blame others, are very likely to get another attack because of their morbid thinking. But if these persons, after the first attack, change their values and religious views, try to improve their relationships with others, take better care of their bodies and reduce the stress in their lives, they will have not only benefited from the heart attack but may also have improved their chance of not getting another one.

• Advance information about one's condition does help. For example, before going for an operation, a prior knowledge about what to expect during and after surgery makes the experience of pain less and enables one to handle the discomfort of surgery more effectively.

• If you are suffering from a chronic illness like arthritis, the best thing is to learn to accept it and live with it as best as you can. Chronic pain can easily cause anxiety and anxiety in turn can stimulate pain. One way to control and eliminate this vicious circle is to change one's attitudes, views and behaviour.

WHAT IS HEALTH?

Health is more than freedom from physical pain. It is the sense of well-being at a profound spiritual and emotional level. When Jesus was on earth, he cured physical illness, but the sick found wholeness of a new kind, because what happens in our body is coloured by what is going on in the rest of us. This wholeness helps us to accept our pain without bitterness, to live lives full of meaning. It shows positive ways through difficult situations and gives strength to bear the pain.

Being on guard

• Against giving in to well-intentioned deception. Some sick persons, because they want to reassure themselves and prevent worry, pretend they are okay, while actually fearing the worst. One must resist this tendency to avoid, deny or suppress the painful side of life, because it may lead to physical, emotional or spiritual disaster.

• Against the tendency to withdraw from others while you are sick, in an attitude of self-pity. A healthier attitude would be to allow others to help us and to love us when we are sick. Loneliness will make illness only more unpleasant.

• Against anger and fights. Because you cannot fight against your illness, you may direct your anger towards your doctor, nurse or even your family members, by releasing it through criticisms, complaints, noisy protests and unreasonable demands. By doing so, you will only frustrate yourself more, besides frustrating others around you.

• Against the tendency to exaggerate the symptoms of your illness. Normally the sick receive more attention and sympathy from others and even an opportunity to be left alone without any responsibility. But this does not mean that we should take advantage of others' kindness by intentionally fabricating our illness with a view to getting more benefits from being sick. By doing so, we only prevent ourselves from getting better.

• Against a 'What's the use?' attitude and going into a coma of inactivity and melancholic brooding. That will only hinder fast recovery. Develop a more balanced view of your present condition: for example, because you have lost your gall bladder, it does not mean you have also lost your mind. Therefore, even if you have a permanent handicap, you can still live a full life with what is left, such as your mental abilities, opportunities and other physical capacities.

• Against resentment of your illness itself, for that will cause anxiety and stress, which can sometimes be even more damaging in their effect than the original disease.

• Against being secretive about your illness. Concerns that are not shared can fester and complicate both the illness and the recovery process.

HANDY TIPS

• Breathe deeply and relax. Become conscious of the presence of God. Say to yourself: "God is full of love for me, he cares for me, he wants to heal and support me." Become aware of any pain or distress you may be feeling and hold them before God.

• Ask yourself what are the things your illness has asked you to sacrifice: a sense of well-being, an attractive look, certain pet hobbies, your job or some relationships? Bring each loss to awareness; imagine that you hold them in your hands, and let each loss go saying, "Go to God from whom you came and come back to me when he sends you again."

• Make a list, if you can, of the changes in your attitudes and lifestyle that the illness is asking of you. Look at each of them and ask yourself whether these changes would bring you better health and lead you to a fuller life. Remember, illness has its bright side, for it could be the vehicle of new life for you.

• Have a crucifix in front of you. Hold it if possible and say to Jesus, "Lord, you experienced during your life, suffering and death. Your suffering redeemed me and the world. I unite my sufferings with yours, so that mine too may become redemptive."

A LITTLE TRICK

Carlo Caretto is a life-long sufferer. In his book *Why Lord?* he offers a trick for coping with pain: **Pray** a simple prayer, remembering that 'help comes to me from the Lord who made heaven and earth'. **Find** some act of love to perform in words or in actions. **Wait**: for 'it is good to wait in silence for God to save'. "Then, I usually fall asleep, so I don't know what happens next. But – at last – I feel better."

HIS WORD COMFORTS

"'Rabbi, who sinned, this man or his parents, that he should have been born blind?' 'Neither he nor his parents sinned,' Jesus answered, 'he was born blind so that the works of God might be revealed in him.'" (Jn 9:2-3)

We are punished more by our sins than for them; sin is such that by its very nature you can no more extract blessedness out of sin than you can suck health out of poison. But this does not mean that when we are sick we should think that God is punishing us for our sins. This feeling of guilt and fear of punishment can grow intense if no recovery is in sight. We need to have a correct understanding of sin and sickness. It is true that, as the Bible states, all sickness comes ultimately because of the Fall. But Jesus clearly taught us that sickness does not always come as the result of individual sins. Sometimes physical illness and personal sins are related but one cannot conclude that individual cases of sickness are necessarily the result of the sick person's sin.

"How rich and deep are the wisdom and the knowledge of God! We cannot reach to the root of his decisions or his ways." (Rom 11:33)

We may not know why God sends us sickness. In fact no one knows why there is suffering in the world. But what we do know is that God's ways are often beyond the capacity of our ability to understand. Hence, have faith. I am not saying you should believe that instant health will always come to those whose faith is strong. No, God has never promised to heal all our diseases in this life. But believe that in God's plan there is a good purpose for your illness. "If I had not any faith," said St Thérèse of Lisieux, "I would have committed suicide without an instant's hesitation." In fact, she even warned the Sisters of her community not to leave anything poisonous nearby! Because faith sees the invisible and believes the unbelievable, it receives the impossible. Because faith listens only to God, it draws poison from every grief, takes the sting from every loss and quenches the fire of every pain.

"Be brave, take heart, all who put your hope in God."
(Ps 31:24)

True faith is never found alone; it is always accompanied by hope. When hope animates us there is vigour in the whole body. It sustains us especially in difficulties. Patients in hospital have been seen to get along better when there is at least a glimmer of hope in them. Therefore, hope that something unforeseen may happen, that you may have a remission or you may live longer than expected, because a loving sovereign God is in charge of the universe. If you hope, you will be brave because bravery is like love; it must have hope for nourishment. This is bravery in man: to bear unflinchingly what heaven sends. Sometimes even to live is an act of bravery, but it is much more true when you are sick. If you hope, you will not only be brave but patient, and patience achieves more than force.

"Passing through the Valley of Weeping they make it a place of springs." (Ps 84:6)

Illness can be a door-opening experience. Saints like Ignatius of Loyola turned their life around after long and serious illness. Ignatius learnt from his illness what was most essential in life: love of neighbour and of God. He spent months recovering from injuries which he sustained in a battle. He remarked, "In these afflictions … I can feel no sadness or pain because I realise that the servant of God, through an illness, turns out to be something of a doctor for the direction and ordering of his life to God's glory and service." Yes, illness refines our faith and opens our soul to God. Sometimes, nothing can so pierce the soul as the uttermost sigh of the body. Illness teaches us to be more compassionate and caring. It shatters the illusion that man is sufficient to himself without God. Of all the parts of the human body, the abdomen is the most alarming when it gets sick. I should think the abdomen alone can be reason enough why a man should not easily take himself for a god! If illness does no other good to us, it at least achieves this: we are fond of one another because our ailments are the same.

A PRAYER

Jesus my healer, I am a vessel broken by
ill-health,
shattered by loss, emptied of ambitions and
strivings.
Fill the cracks of pain in this vessel, with your
love;
the gashes of frustration with hope;
and the holes of despair with your healing.

In health, I forgot you, but in sickness I come
*   back to you.*
Hang on to me, Lord,
because I am not well enough to hang on to you.

"Heal me O Lord, and I shall be healed; save me,
and I shall be saved." (Jer 17:14)

"Bless the Lord, O my soul, let all that is
*   within me*
bless his holy name, for he forgives all your sins,
and heals all your diseases." (Ps 103:1-3)

7

WHEN AGEING

"Don't past tense me"

Age is the only thing that comes to us without effort. Whether we want it or not, we grow old. A person can defy even death but not his age. Only in heaven all would live long and none would be old. However, growing old need not scare us, for it can be a new venture in itself. Many who are old find their souls opening up like roses, not closing up like cabbages. Pope John XXIII became Pope at the age of 77. His dynamic leadership set in motion the Second Vatican Council. In our youth-oriented society, older adults are made to feel their usefulness ends at 65, if not sooner. Many old people call it a nonsense and go right on leading productive lives. Productive older persons may retire from their jobs but they refuse to retire from life. Picasso was still producing drawings at 90, and his paintings became more innovative with the years. Douglas McArthur became commander of the United Nations Forces at 70. Winston Churchill continued to influence the world as an elderly British statesman. One must not think that these are famous exceptions, because there are thousands who never become famous but show that later years need not be times of misery, rigidity and inactivity. They consider their old age a triumphant and satisfying reality. They would resent a pitying attitude towards them, for they are finding a fulfilment for life that they have long deserved, with inner resources to meet it with joy and usefulness. When someone told the 89-year-old poet Dorothy Duncan that she had lived a full life, she responded tartly, "Don't past tense me."

"The best is yet to be"

There is no age that can be called the best age, though some would swear that the best age is marriage. In fact, the best in everyone's life is still waiting to come. So, Robert Browning invites his readers to "Grow old with me! The best is yet to be." Those who enter into their old age with this hope will only look at the bright side of their age and enjoy it. Old age has a great sense of calm; when the passions release their hold, we are released from the grasp of many masters. As the seas are quiet when the winds give over, so are we calm when passions are no more. Old age brings with it freedom: freedom to enjoy special interests, to set your own goals and pace and to reach out to others in new directions. With old age comes a chance to learn a new set of attitudes towards life, as it is possible to teach old dogs new tricks. Old age opens opportunities to start a second career, to launch into voluntary work, to start new hobbies and to educate oneself in new fields. In fact, the older years give opportunity for many of the interests and activities that younger years had to postpone.

Yes, it has problems

Old age itself is not a problem. It is just a fact that you were born a long time ago. But as every age has some problems, so does old age. If one wants to go to a place where there are no problems, one can: it is called a cemetery.

• Physically, there is increased limitation of strength. You have reached old age when you are willing to get up and give your seat to a lady on the bus and you can't.

• Mentally there is a decline in mental ability which is most apparent when one has to make a quick decision, like stepping on the brakes or jumping out of danger. Years steal fire from the mind and vigour from the limbs.

• Socially, the self-confidence and self-esteem of older people are often undermined by the prejudices of those who think that the elderly are too old to be of any use and hence treat them as unimportant.

• For many old persons, there is a devastating loss of social contact. Years bring the death of old friends and one is left to murmur with the poet: "They are all gone into the world of light and I alone sit lingering here."

• Retirement brings departure from work but for many it also brings a low income, a reduced standard of living. For some others, the inability to accept retirement is itself a problem.

• There are fears which many older persons have to live with: the fear of the complete reordering of life, the fear of long illness with the thought of outliving financial resources, the fear of becoming a burden to others, the fear of the experience of death, questions about immortality as well as feelings of guilt and remorse and concern about the unfinished tasks of life.

Yet, it is encouraging

In spite of the problems unique to old age, several surveys offer encouragement to the older person:
• At least half of all people between 75 and 84, are free of health problems that require special care.
• Many problems once thought to be caused by age are really caused by poor health habits. A balanced diet and regular exercise can improve health at any age. Even with serious health problems, life can be productive and happy.
• Most older persons are prone to arthritis, high blood pressure, hearing impairment or heart disease – but these are physical impairments to which many people adapt without much decline in activity.
• Although the peak of physical accomplishment may have passed for the older person, the quality of one's spiritual life and the insight of one's mind can continue to increase.
• With age the power of the mind can decline, yet older persons with their wisdom and some extra effort can continue to be creative and able to learn in their later years.

Taking care

• Bored by the inactivity of retirement, saddened by the death of friends and other such frustrations, older persons can easily daydream about the "good old days" as if there was nothing painful or unpleasant in the past. Such a retreat sometimes contributes to confusion and mental infirmity.

• Because of the loss of social contacts, old persons are inclined to withdraw from society altogether and into feeling that they are no longer useful or needed, which might contribute in some cases to premature death.

• People differ in the way they adjust to retirement. Some welcome retirement and are able to relax and enjoy their golden years. Others, unable or unwilling to face the realities of age, react with anger, condemn themselves, and blame others for their miseries. Such persons often slide into depression.

• Today the older person is also forced to deal with the problem of negative stereotypes. Our culture has led us to believe from youth that old people are weak, forgetful and senile, so that, as we get older, we begin looking for signs that we are falling apart, when in fact we may be getting stronger.

• There should be an honest facing of the changes that old age brings. We cannot fight against inevitable realities. We have to accept them and grow through them.

HANDY TIPS

• Acknowledge that you are ageing and the losses involved in your ageing and accept all of the accompanying feelings. Write a list of all that you have gained and lost, as you have aged. Willingly let go the losses; picture yourself taking each loss into your hands and setting it free, saying, "I'm grateful for all the gifts you have given me and in the name of my growth in this life, I set you free and send you back to God from whom you came."

• When reminiscing about your past, avoid focusing on your past failures, guilt and fears; rather, consider your accomplishments and get a more balanced perspective on both the past and the present.

• Join informal groups of elderly people like yourself. It can give you contacts with others, acceptance and assurance that your problems are not unique or abnormal.

• You can avoid some of the problems of old age, if you keep using your mind in some useful activity, exercising your body, regulating your diet, making good use of your leisure time and finding creative ways of serving others.

• Learn, however late in life, that burning up energy in anxiety will not do any good; learn to manage tension; learn that self-pity and resentment are the most toxic of drugs; learn to bear the things you can't change.

HIS WORD COMFORTS

"Now I am old, but ever since my youth, I never saw an upright person abandoned or the descendants of the upright forced to beg their food." (Ps 37:25)

Worry seems to be a welcome companion to the old. As we grow old our worries increase: worry about the past, the present and particularly the future. Will my children come to visit me at all? Will there be anyone around me when I'm sick? Will my pension be further diminished? Most older persons worry about their health. My grandfather in his advanced age worried so much about his health that all the phone numbers in his little black book were doctors. One evil in old age is that you think that every little illness is the beginning of the end; of course, when a man expects to be arrested, every knock at the door is an alarm. The fact of the matter is that many of the things we worry about never happen. Worry is like a rocking chair; it will give you something to do, but it won't get you anywhere. Hence, never trouble trouble, till trouble troubles you. Instead of worrying about tomorrow, take each day as it comes; each day brings opportunities and privileges that will not be repeated. One should trust in God's providence which cares for young and old. God makes a promise, but do we have faith to believe it, hope to anticipate it, patience to await it? He who gives us teeth, will he not give us bread? The beginning of worry is the end of faith and the beginning of faith is the end of worry.

"But to prove to you that the Son of man has authority on earth to forgive sins – Jesus said to the paralytic: 'Get up, pick up your bed and go off home.' And the man got up and went home." (Mt 9:6)

As we get older, we probably feel that our body is declining faster than it should, and we feel that it is partly because in the past we had mistreated it by some sinful habits and abused it – perhaps by too much smoking, eating or alcoholic consumption. Yes, it is possible that man could live twice as long if he didn't spend the first half of his life acquiring habits that shorten the other half. So we feel guilty and a guilty conscience needs no accuser, whereas a quiet conscience can sleep well even in thunder. But we can remove our guilt and restore peace to our soul by seeking forgiveness for our past from Jesus who has authority on earth to forgive sins. He does not forgive piecemeal or in instalments but blasts the whole guilt at once, and by his forgiveness what is broken is made whole and what is soiled is made clean.

"I am the resurrection. Anyone who believes in me, even though that person dies, will live." (Jn 11:25)

Old age, declining health and the passing of friends all bring us face to face with the reality of death. Perhaps one is afraid of dying and worried about what is going to happen after death. Yes, the thought of death can be fearsome, for it is the final and painful departure from this world. Not all the preaching since Adam has made death other than death. But one cannot forget that it is as natural to die as to be born. All human beings are subject to decay; when God summons, even monarchs must obey. However, to a believer death is not the end but a beginning to eternal life. At baptism we were reborn in Christ and hence, if we share in his death we will also rise from the dead to share his new life. This belief in our resurrection is not an appendage to the Christian faith, it *is* the Christian faith. Hence, by constantly worrying over death, do not seek death – death will find you anyway! Rather, seek the road which makes death a fulfilment.

"Let anyone who is thirsty come to me! Let anyone who believes in me come and drink." (Jn 7:38)

Perhaps the mundane activities of our middle age have crowded out from our life some of the idealism and spiritual interests that our youth had known. Perhaps the preoccupations of our past life have obscured the more important spiritual values and now we feel that we cannot any more be satisfied by the trivial and material but must seek to deepen our spiritual life.

Fortunately, old age with its retirement offers us time and opportunity for spiritual rebuilding, while Jesus the fountain of living water is with us offering spiritual nourishment to satisfy all our thirsts. Hence, approach him frequently through prayer, the word of God, and the sacraments, to receive his divine grace; when grace is joined with wrinkles it is adorable, for it brings an unspeakable dawn in happy old age. The more we come to Christ, the more we become Christlike, which is a good preparation for eternal life. A dear old lady was asked what she used to preserve her charms. She replied sweetly: "I use for the lips, truth; for the voice, prayer; for the eyes, pity; for the hands, charity; for the figure, uprightness; and for the heart, love."

"I have loved you with an everlasting love and so I still maintain my faithful love for you." (Jer 31:3)

In our culture, age is what makes antiques worth more, but people worth less. Modern culture seems to think that if you get past the age of 80, you are a maintenance problem. Hence now that we are old, everything around us is perhaps letting us know that we are not terribly important any more, that we are just a lot of trouble and that we are just not as valuable as all other people. But don't be disheartened by this cultural bias. It is a prejudice that denounces old age, discriminates against the elderly and assumes that 'the younger is better'. On our part, we must hold on to our self-esteem as a person and a Christian. The true measure of a person is not his age but the height of his ideals, the breath of his sympathy, the depth of his convictions and the length of his patience. As a Christian you are a beloved child of God and as his child you are an heir of God and co-heir with Christ to the riches of God's Kingdom. That is why God loves you and me with an everlasting love. He loves you in days of calm or days of storm; his love is the same whether you are young or old, a love that ever gives, forgives and outlives.

A PRAYER

Eternal yet ageless God!
You love me with an eternal love, holding my
*   hand*
as I struggle through every stage of my life.
You alone steer my boat through all its journey,
but have a more special care of it,
when it comes to a narrow current
or to a dangerous fall of waters.
Now that old age has seized upon me,
the signs of age have begun to mark my body
and the illness that is to carry me off has finally
begun to strike from without and within me;
cast me not away, O Lord, but let your strength
be made perfect in my weakness.
Open your eyes wider and enlarge your
*   providence,*
so that no illness or agony may shake my spirit.
Cleanse in me what I cannot cleanse,
mend in me what I cannot mend.

*Assist me to be wise from the experience of
    the past
and to move into the future with joy and hope;
be to me a sure and certain hope of the life
that you have prepared for me in heaven.*

8

WHEN FEELING GUILTY

James needed a watch. He went to a jewellery shop. As he was trying on some expensive watches, the assistant was called to the other side of the counter. It happened so fast, he couldn't believe that he had done it. He just slipped one of the watches into his inside pocket. He was sure that the assistant never knew one was gone since there were many more watches in the showcase. And once he'd done it, there was no way he could undo it, because the assistant would know. He waited, looked around and got out of the store as fast as he could. But he began to feel guilty. A guilty conscience needs no accuser, whereas a quiet conscience can sleep even in thunder. "I am a thief," he often said to himself, "I must be a terrible person; I've never stolen anything before but now I have done it." Since every guilty person is his own hangman, James was continually feeling mental and spiritual anguish, so much that all of his life became miserable. So he hid the watch away in the bottom of his chest of drawers, thinking that later he would find a way to slip it into the store's showcase without anyone noticing it. Eventually he sent cash to the store with a note that it was for something taken. Even then his guilty feeling would not allow him to wear the stolen watch. He went to confession but still he felt so guilty that whenever he went shopping in any store, he was a nervous wreck, afraid he would steal something again.

A life-disrupting force

Along with our ability to do good, we all have a comparable capacity to do evil, with the result that all of us often suffer from guilt. Guilt is at the basis of much human suffering. The experience of guilt is nearly always a part of people's other difficulties, such as depression, loneliness, grief, marriage break-downs and many other problems. Guilt can be a life-disrupting force. A sense of guilt makes a person allergic even to a direct honest gaze. Those who feel guilty are afraid and those who are afraid somehow feel guilty. Suspicion always haunts the guilty. The evil-doer flees when no man pursues, while the righteous are as bold as a lion. A sense of guilt can also easily contaminate society and encourage in others the very type of behaviour that can further increase guilt feelings. Guilt feelings actually prove the saying that you cannot do wrong without suffering wrong.

What is guilt?

When people talk about guilt, they usually refer to *subjective* guilt feelings. But there is also *objective* guilt.

Objective guilt occurs when a law has been broken. It could be the violation of God's law, or of society's law for example by stealing from a department store; or it could be the violation of a standard which a person has set for himself. For example, a father who determines to spend each Sunday with the family, experiences guilt if he fails to do it. It could be also the breaking of an unwritten but socially expected rule, for example by gossiping maliciously.

Subjective guilt is the uncomfortable feeling of regret, remorse and self-condemnation, which comes when we have done something wrong or have failed to do something right. Subjective guilt is *false,* if our guilt feelings are out of proportion to the seriousness of the act. It is *true,* if the guilt feeling is the result of the violation of a law, and if it fits in with the action.

Taking care

Objective guilt can be harmful: If a legal law is broken, arrest and conviction may follow; if a social expectation is violated, it may bring people's criticism; if one's own personal standard is violated, it leads to self-condemnation; if God's law is broken, the Bible says that death is the punishment, although God pardons and gives eternal life to a repentant sinner.

Subjective guilt feelings can cause further damage:
• Instead of admitting that we have done something wrong and asking God to forgive us, we may attempt other improper ways of reducing the feelings of guilt, such as blaming others, denying any wrongdoing, or justifying the wrong.
• If guilt is not properly dealt with, the guilt feeling may lead one to self-condemnation, self-punishment, and feelings of inferiority.
• When guilt feelings are allowed to accumulate over the years, they can produce physical tension. If

you blame yourself for a long time, your body begins to deteriorate and eventually breaks down.

• Guilt feelings can often remain suppressed and can do much harm, and there is a way to discover the suppressed feeling: persons who have suppressed guilt are usually on the defensive, unconsciously working at protecting themselves from exposure of their guilt.

• If a person thinks his guilt can never be wiped out or that he can never undo the pain his wrong deeds have caused to others, he begins to live in profound moral distress, carrying the emotional scars, perhaps, all through his life.

• True guilt is a moral issue and guilt feelings result from moral failures. Therefore, psychological treatments to remove the guilt feelings are not enough; they are at best stopgap efforts that rarely seem to bring permanent change. In order to have radical treatment for the guilt, one must acknowledge the central place of sin and seek forgiveness.

HEALING GUILT FEELINGS

If guilt is false

• An individual's standards of what is right and wrong, good and bad, usually develop in childhood, set by one's parents or teachers. In some homes, the standards are so rigid and so high that they are impossible for the child to reach. Yet, the growing children come to accept the standards of their parents and expect perfection in themselves. If they fail, they feel guilty. The best way to deal with guilt feelings arising out of unrealistic standards is to re-examine them and adopt realistic standards.

• Social pressure can create guilt feelings. Our perception of ourselves is greatly influenced by the opinions and criticisms of others. In everyday life, we are continually soaked in the unhealthy atmosphere of mutual criticism. Every reproach evokes feelings of guilt. The right response to guilt feelings arising out of social suggestions is to develop one's own mind on moral issues, and the strength of character to stand by one's convictions, even in the face of criticisms from others.

• False guilt feelings may arise from a faulty conscience. If a person has been taught from childhood to feel guilty for what is not wrong in the eyes of God; if one violates God's law due to ignorance of what is right and wrong, an ignorance one can't avoid; if the conscience has been blinded through the habit of committing sins. In all such cases, one's conscience can be said to have gone astray and hence needs moral re-education.

• Satan too can cause false guilt feelings. He can attempt to intervene in our lives both before and after sin. He can stimulate believers to continue feeling guilty and unforgiven, even when we have done nothing wrong or have been forgiven by God.

If guilt is true

Admitting: If you are not guilty of any sin but feel guilty, you are believing a lie, condemning yourself for nothing. But if you believe that you are truly guilty of some wrongdoing, acknowledge it. By acknowledging our failures we are moving through them, stronger, towards a better and fuller life. Acknowledge also the accompanying guilt feelings.

In themselves true guilt feelings may not be that bad. Sometimes, they stimulate us to confess our sins and act more effectively.

Confessing: If you have actually hurt someone terribly, go and say sorry. If you have harmed some public group by thoughtless words or deeds, say so publicly. If you believe in the Sacrament of confession, in some cases it might be helpful to confess your sins to a priest.

Repenting: Repentance is not simply being sorry for sin, but being sorry for the deep self-centred attitude that has led to sin. Let this sorrow be constructive, not just remorse. Constructive sorrow leads to constructive change. Make a firm decision to alter your attitude and behaviour. By changing them with God's grace, you will avoid repeating the deed and regretting it. Ask forgiveness from God. Remember that the person who seeks forgiveness must be genuinely repentant and willing to forgive others.

Believing: Believe that God has forgiven you. The guilt feelings may not disappear overnight, but be assured that your sins are forgiven, even if you don't feel that they have been. The concern of God is not to fill us with a sense of guilt but to use the feeling of guilt as a door, opening on to new opportunities of fuller life.

HIS WORD COMFORTS

"'Neither do I condemn you,' said Jesus to the woman; 'go away, and from this moment sin no more.'"

(Jn 8:11)

Knowing fully well that sin has made us all mad as well as bad, some people still deny sin. Jesus did not condemn the woman caught in adultery but neither did he condone sin; he told her to sin no more. In the Bible, there appears to be little difference between sin and guilt. As members of a spoiled race, all of us are sinners. If we had no faults, we would not take so much pleasure in noticing them in others. All of us have an ability to get tangled up, for dust is the origin and earthly end of our body. Sin is not wrong doing, it is wrong being. Sin is not, not doing the will of God, but not choosing the will of God. Sin is the root of guilt feelings. Sin pays – but it pays in remorse and regret. Sin is like a decaying fruit, which can grow only more rotten. Hence, the sooner we get rid of sin the better.

"I heard your voice…, and I was afraid…, and I hid myself." (Gen 3:10)

Even when there is no law, there is conscience. We never do anything, however secret, without the presence of two witnesses: God and our conscience. The conscience acts as the built-in voice of the Creator. It may have strong social relations but it is more than the voice of the crowd. To ignore the voice of the conscience is to forego a peace which is above all earthly dignities. A peaceful conscience can sleep even in the mouth of a cannon. The fear we feel after sinning is not designed to keep us crippled by guilt feelings, but rather to lead us beyond them. God is concerned with our fruitful living and he is anxious to get us on the way towards it. Whatever may be the moral values we have inherited from others in childhood, as adults we have a moral obligation to develop a mature conscience. An infantile conscience may often be quiet, but never secure. The mature conscience does not seek religious justification for its warped values, but finds its justification always through a right relationship with God. The mature conscience can still make mistakes, but it is able to take the consequences and grow through errors.

"If we confess our sins, he is faithful and just and will forgive our sins, and cleanse us from all evil." (1 Jn 1:9)

Jesus has atoned for all our sins but we have to claim it through repenting, confessing and receiving forgiveness. To repent is to feel constructive sorrow, which is not same as guilt feelings. Suppose I spill coffee on someone's lap. A guilt-feeling reaction would be: "How stupid I am. Look at the mess I have made. I am sorry." But the reaction of constructive sorrow would be: "I'm very sorry. Let me help you to wipe it up." In confession, we acknowledge our faults in order to repair by our sincerity the damage they have done to ourselves and to others. Confession of our faults is the next thing to innocence, because when we uncover our sin, God covers it, and when we confess, God pardons. Yet how difficult we find it to confess our faults! How easily sin gets into my heart, and how hardly it gets out of my mouth!

"We had all gone astray, each in his own way; but God brought the acts of rebellion of all of us to bear upon him (Jesus)." (Is 53:6)

Sin cannot be undone, only forgiven, and God forgives if we seek forgiveness. I have a book on my left hand. Let my left hand represent you and the book represent your sin. Where is your sin now? Of course, it is "on you". Now I take the book from my left hand and place it on my right hand. Let my right hand represent Christ. Where is your sin now? Obviously, it is "on Christ". God did exactly this with all our sins. He laid them all on Christ who atoned for them with his blood. Therefore ask God to forgive and believe he has forgiven you. With this unassailable belief, forget the past. Why remember the past and be sad, when we can forget and smile? It may not be easy, but it is easier than allowing our past to ruin our future. Forgetting the past, strain forward to what lies ahead, setting a worthy purpose for your life, a purpose worthy enough to engage your whole being in creative living.

A PRAYER

Lord Jesus, I feel fragmented within me;
I have gone in many directions at once and
sinned;
some sins are plain to me, some escape me,
some other sins, I cannot face:
the wrong desires of my heart, the sinful
devisings of my mind and the corrupt use of
my body!
I have sought opposite goals in contradictory
ways;
I preached justice but walked in injustice,
I shouted peace but practised violence,
I prayed for life but traded in death.
Light a candle in my heart, that I may see more!
You who drew out a fountain of water in the
desert,

draw from the hardness of my heart tears of
*   sorrow.*
Forgive me, and hold not my sins against me.
In your great tenderness, soothe away my faults.
Your kindness alone can restore my brokenness,
your grace alone can calm my agitation,
your power alone can strengthen my frailty.
Give me new life, for I am worn and tired;
give me new love, for I have turned hard-hearted.
May the oil of your anointing
penetrate the cells of my being;
may the warmth of your touch
steady me and give me courage,
to walk through the desert sands of guilt
*   and pain,*
to the living water of peace and joy.

9

WHEN ADDICTED

A major problem

Addiction is a major problem today. An addiction is any thinking or behaviour that is habitual, repetitious and difficult or impossible to control. Some are addicted to substances such as drugs, alcohol, cigarettes or even to pot, cocaine or marijuana. I was once in a drugstore and overheard this: "You should cut out these pills, they could be habit forming," said the pharmacist. "Nonsense," replied the customer, "I've been taking them for twelve years." The only thing some people can fix around their house are Scotch and Martinis, and they always wake up at the crack of ice. A friend of mine read in the *Reader's Digest* that cigarettes are bad for you; so he gave up reading the *Reader's Digest*. Some are addicted to smoking opium; don't they know that to smoke opium is like getting out of the train while it is still running? Some get addicted to certain behaviour such as gambling, watching television or working. Gambling is pretty much like liquor – you can make it illegal but you can't make it unpopular. Some may hate television as much as they hate spinach, but they can't stop eating spinach. Some become workaholics, as if God punished us with work, when in fact he blessed us with it. It is good for all of us to know that substances such as drugs or alcohol may give a temporary feeling of euphoria but they never solve problems nor reduce tension, rather they only create additional stress. There are, of course, medical treatments and counselling methods available to enable people to withdraw from addictive substances and to heal the effects of addiction. These include individual and group counselling, drug education, residential therapy, family counselling and after-care services. But to prevent addiction, one has to be first aware of its dangers.

Pain and pathos

Drugs: When I buy a pill, I buy also a kind of peace, but I get conditioned to cheap solutions instead of deeper ones. Addiction to strong drugs can seriously damage one's mind and body for ever. Some new wonder drugs are so powerful that you have to be in perfect health to take them. Pot, for example, is like a gang of bandits in your brain, who tie your thoughts up and trash them.

Alcohol: There is a difference between alcohol, alcoholism and alcohol abuse. *Alcohol* is a drug which has a mood-altering ingredient in it; its use often precedes the use of other drugs. Large quantities of it interfere with our sanity and sound outlook. That is why in a pub, nobody cares about how your English is provided your Scotch is good, and a man who enters a pub optimistically often comes out very pessimistically. *Alcoholism* is a chronic, progressive and potentially dangerous disease to oneself and to society, which can be arrested only by complete abstinence. Alcoholism is no spectator sport; eventually the whole family gets to play. How many deaths are caused by drunken driving! Some drunken drivers are in the habit of taking a curve at high speed when there is none. One reason why the courts don't handle more drunken driver cases is that the undertaker gets them first. *Alcohol abuse* is a problem with alcohol, even in one who may not be an alcoholic; it can cause serious health problems even before one becomes alcoholic.

Smoking: Smoking certainly shortens your cigarettes, but it can also shorten your life. The family who smokes together, chokes together.

Gambling: Gambling is like diving into an empty swimming pool – the chances of hitting the bottom are about the same. It is the sure way of getting nothing for something.

Television: One has to be aware that television is no more what it once was – a small box containing entertainment, news, sport; it is now often a window opening on to a violent world, encouraging a sleazy way of life.

Work: Too many of us worship work. An intemperance in work can be as harmful as in drink. God gave us work for our livelihood but for the sake of getting a livelihood, we shouldn't forget to live.

A disease or a sin?

Is addiction a disease or a sin? Some say that it is a disease because it is predictable, progressive but treatable. The addicts may differ in their symptoms but all show physical symptoms and psychological difficulties and their behaviour disrupts their social and work life. Others say that addiction, as a social phenomenon and a behaviour disorder, is a clear evidence of sin. That is why many addicts feel in their guts that theirs is a self-inflicted moral problem. But in this chapter we assume that addiction is both a sickness and a sin. It is true that some persons are physiologically more prone to become addicts to certain things than others. However, there is always a point of time when every drinker makes his or her decision to take a first drink and, at least in the initial stage, every drinker is free to decide to stop or to continue. Therefore, addiction is also a moral condition and an addict is at least partially responsible for his addiction.

Where from? – How one gets addicted

• Drug addiction can be caused by parental and other adult examples. Drugs in themselves are not bad and there is no harm in the occasional use of mild sedatives to relieve pain or to relax. But children who see adults taking pills regularly will conclude that a pill is a way out of difficulties and eventually follow the elders' example.
• Children who grow up in an alcoholic home environment are often confused, angry, scared and feel guilty and hence they eventually join other adult children of alcoholics.
• Many alcoholic families tend to perpetuate the drinking problem at home. As long as the family tries to deny that such a problem exists at home, not caring if a member drinks, hiding it from others, and even protecting the drinker from the consequences of his or her irresponsible behaviour, the problem is perpetuated.
• Drug or alcoholic addiction can be caused by peer

influence. Peers can shape attitudes about drugs and provide social context for drug use. Pressure from peers, the desire to experiment in getting drunk, and a belief that alcohol use will prove his manhood, and enable him to get even with his parents – all these may pave the way for a teenager to become alcoholic.

• Cultural expectations in a given society can drag people to addiction. For example, a culture that is tolerant of drunkenness, that encourages adults to get 'high' as if it is the 'in' thing to do, and that uses terms like 'happy hour' or 'Christmas cheer' to describe alcohol use, provides conditions ripe for alcohol abuse.

• Behaviour addictions such as gambling, work-aholism or shoplifting sometimes have a physical base and need medical treatment. But more often, they have psychological and spiritual roots which cannot be easily identified. These addicts just thrive on danger and excitement, interspersed, of course, with bouts of depression and stress.

• In general, a spiritual void leads people to fill it in with smaller gods. The route to addiction is made easier when a person has lost spiritual and moral values. If there is no religious belief or moral instruction, materialism and personal pleasure take their place.

RECOVERY TIPS

From behavioural addiction

Determination: Take a decision to change. A one-off decision may not be enough. Since addictive behaviour is pleasurable, don't be surprised if you relapse into it again. What is needed is that you make a decision again and again, but every time with greater determination.

Replacement: Whenever an unwanted thought comes to awareness, think STOP and even say this out loud. But as soon as the unwanted thinking is interrupted, quickly switch your mind to some other healthy thought.

Need fulfilment: Being addicted to something un-desirable is a sign that some need is not being met in more healthy ways. For example, if you are a compulsive television watcher, perhaps you need contact with other human beings but are afraid of intimacy.

From substance addiction

• Admit that you are addicted but you can control it.

• Convince yourself that the time to become free of drugs, including alcohol, is today, and hence join today in a legitimate programme of recovery.

• Work your programme step by step for recovery can be a life-long process.

• Do not try it by yourself, but get help from a qualified person.

• Do not give up the effort if you relapse. Keep giving yourself another chance, as God does with us.

• Besides your effort, seek strength and power from God to be drug-free.

• Stay away not only from all alcohol, but also from alcohol-using friends.

• You may be tempted to use alcohol again. But remember temptation is no sin; falling into it is what matters.

- Be aware of the human tendency to lie to yourself by rationalising wrong behaviour.
- Pride goes before destruction; do not become proud if you become alcohol free.
- Have confidence in God. Walk with God one day at a time, holding his hand and living always in his presence.
- Seek guidance for your life in the Bible, the Word of God.
- Attend church worship regularly, for worship leads you to serve God and others.
- Join some Christian groups with whom you can share your problems and receive support, encouragement and advice.

HIS WORD COMFORTS

"True, for me everything is permissible, but I am determined not to be dominated by anything." (1 Cor 6:12)

The golden saying, that he who conquers himself conquers the world, must be taken seriously by all. If I want to be superior to external influences, I must first become superior to my own passions and not be dominated by them. We often think that we should not allow ourselves to be enslaved only by bad actions. But the fact is that we can be mastered to our own great detriment even by things and actions that are permissible and not bad in themselves. For example, food, sex and even some drugs are good in themselves until we become conquered by them. He who conquers others may be strong, but he who conquers himself is mighty.

"The grace of God has taught us that we should give up everything contrary to true religion and all our worldly passions. We must be self-restrained and live upright and religious lives in this present world." (Tit 2:12)

Self-restraint is self-control and without self-control, a man digs his own grave, because there is a raging tiger inside everyone of us; the sooner we build inside ourselves a cage, and pen that tiger in, the better. The tiger is my ego, wounded by sin and yet craving for what is sinful, which makes a mystery of us all. As believers, we are expected to say no to ungodliness and worldly appetites. Uncontrolled self-indulgence can kill the body as well as the spirit. Self-control is one of the fruits of the Spirit and hence one needs to seek help from God to be self-restrained. One might as well try to catch sunbeams with a fishhook as try to control the self unassisted by the Spirit.

"Do not get drunk with wine, for many evils lie along the path; be filled with the Holy Spirit and controlled by him." (Eph 5:18)

Though it be disfigured by many defects, to whom is his own body not dear? What is more important in life than our bodies, or in the world than what we look like? To a Christian believer in particular, if anything is sacred our human bodies are sacred, because they were created and redeemed by God, made into the temples of the Holy Spirit through baptism and are destined for final resurrection. Hence we are expected to glorify God also with our bodies, by keeping them pure, free from every kind of pollutants such as drugs, alcohol, evil thoughts, excessive food and the like. When the dignity of our body is rejected, neglected or abused, the Gospel of Christ is not put into action.

"Never worry about anything; but tell God all your desires of every kind in prayer and petition, shot through with gratitude and the peace of God which is beyond our understanding will guard your hearts and your thoughts in Christ Jesus." (Phil 4:6)

Our faith in God has to be big. If it is small we will be seeking after only small things such as food, drink and clothes, and in so doing we will miss the real meaning of life and start asking, "Is life worth living?", which is a question for an embryo, not for a man. But those with big faith in God, who put him above everything else, will charge their minds with meaning which they never had before. They will walk with God day by day through prayer, in the conviction that life on earth is good but eternal life is better. Such persons will live one day at a time, free of yesterday, unburdened by tomorrow and filled with assurance for today, in the belief that this life is only a childhood of our immortality.

"Am I my brother's keeper?" (Gen 4:9)

The chaos of our society began when Cain, after murdering his brother Abel, said to God, "Am I my brother's keeper?", for it was then that man declared himself not responsible for the welfare of the society in which he himself has to live. One wonders, why should our privileges be greater than our obligations to society; is it not the performance of our responsibilities which actually guarantees the protection of our rights? Surely it does. It is the interests of the individual that are threatened, when he, by his addictive behaviour, destroys something or someone, thus causing disintegration of the community. It is not a matter of choice but God's commandment that we curb our self-indulgence that is sure to cause damage to society. Without a sense of responsibility to others, I may have a soft life but it will be boneless and it cannot hold itself together.

A PRAYER

O Living God, I am at the mercy of powers
that grip my self to the point of crisis.
I am drained, I am hurting, I feel miserable.
Addiction has so entered my body
that my nerve to live and to create is breaking;
addiction has so deeply entered into my mind,
that the futility of life oppresses my soul and
I have lost my ability to value what is of value
*   to you.*
I am now left only with a natural passion to
*   express*
the empty void of nothingness through this
*   addictive idol!*
Oh, how I wish to tear this idol apart from
*   your throne*
so that I love and worship you alone!
Let not my slippery footsteps slide; hold me lest
*   I fall.*
Forgive my foolish ways; reclothe me in my
*   rightful mind;*
breathe through the heats of my desire your
*   cooling balm;*
suffer me not so to undervalue my self as to give
*   away my soul,*

your soul, the precious soul, for nothing.
Draw all the fragments of my life
into the bright mosaic of your love.
Cleanse and sweeten the springs of my being;
let your light flow into my conscious mind,
and your grace into my unconscious self.
Keep peace within me and keep turmoil out.
keep strength within me and keep weakness out
To be turned from you is to fall but to turn to
    you is to rise;
so I now stand in your presence to live for ever.

10

WHEN BREAKING UP

"Marriage may be compared to a great tree growing right up through the centre of one's living room. It is huge and wherever one happens to be going – to the fridge, to bed, to the bathroom or out the front door – the tree has to be taken into account. To be married is to be confronted intimately day after day with the mystery of life, of other life, of life outside of oneself. Marriage is one of the great steps we can take in the direction of choosing for ourselves the closeness of God, in the form of a close relationship with another person."
(Mike Mason, *The Mystery of Marriage*)

Many marriages succeed. Thousands of couples are happily married and remain so even in their advanced years. However, quite a few marriages, like flowers, fade away leaving no trace; others yield no fruit and if they do, the fruit does not ripen. Some couples are still legally married and live together but there is no warmth, intimacy or communication between them. When pressures in the family persist, some simply leave their spouses, leaving behind hurt feelings, confusion and a one-parent family. Some young couples enter marriage determined to build a bridge to the moon or at least a palace on earth, but unfortunately they end up building only a watershed. What is more tragic is that some of them give up building anything at all, for they prefer to break away and get divorced. Apart from those times when divorce may seem to be the most feasible alternative to a problem-plagued marriage, divorce can never be a happy solution to a marital problem. Hence, when conflicts set in, instead of breaking away, couples determined to make a success of their marriage will do their best to resolve their differences and continue to live together happily till the end.

Sources of conflict

Social attitudes: Many today see marriage, not as the permanent union created by God but only as a temporary arrangement of convenience. A marriage today can be terminated legally simply on the grounds of 'irreconcilable differences'. These and similar social attitudes and conditions encourage couples to consider divorce as an easy fire-escape.

Inflexibility: Each enters marriage with over two decades of past experiences and ways of looking at things. Each brings into marriage a unique personality together with its differences. These differences can often be complementary. But if each is unwilling to acknowledge the differences, remains insensitive to the other person's point of view and refuses to change in order to accommodate, there is bound to be tension.

Values: What is really important in life? How should we spend time and money? What are our needs and goals? The answers to these questions concern values. When the couples have similar values, the marriage is healthy, but if their values are in conflict, problems arise.

Sexual difficulties: Sexual difficulties can also create tensions. Impatience, frigidity and infidelity seem to be the most common sex problems. Unless they are resolved, the marriage will suffer.

Gender roles: Today, the traditional male–female roles are being re-evaluated. Opinions seem to be changing rapidly about the meaning of husband and wife. If partners have not agreed among themselves as to the nature and extent of their roles, competition and feelings of threat are bound to create tension.

Religion: Religion can be a strengthening force in marriage. But if the spouses differ in their religious interests, in their commitment to spiritual things, and in their denominational preferences, religion can also be a destructive force.

Spiritual vacuum: Marital conflict is often a symptom of something deeper, such as selfishness, lack of love, unwillingness to forgive, and bitterness. These deeper roots can be healed if the couples return to God and develop a consistent relationship with Christ.

Boredom: As years roll by, husbands and wives settle in routines and get accustomed to each other. This often takes away the enthusiasm of early years, making life dull and monotonous, with the result that one or both partners may slip into self-pity or search elsewhere for variety, causing marital tensions.

Preventing conflicts

Be positive: Have a generally positive attitude towards your spouse: view your partner as your best friend and assume that you are married to someone who cares for you.

Be committed: Believe in the importance of marriage. From the beginning, marriage has been viewed as something people should stick with and work to develop in spite of difficulties. Marriage takes time, effort and commitment to grow

Be determined: Have a determination to make the marriage a success. Do not allow work, church or other community responsibilities to take precedence over time spent with your spouse.

Be integrated: Resist the temptation to move and grow through marital life independently of your spouse. Be willing to share confidences and even to be vulnerable in the process. But avoid over-integration. Do not let your relationship become so engulfing that both of you lose your identities, with the result that when something goes wrong, neither of you will own full responsibility for it, but each will say, "I'm not the only one who is guilty."

Be communicative: When you speak define what is important and stress it; be respectful for the other person's worth as a human being; be clear and specific; be realistic and reasonable; ask questions and listen carefully; speak kindly and softly. *Avoid* contradictions: suppose you say to your husband, "I don't mind if you go on the business trip"; but while saying so, you use a slumping posture, resigned tone and a long face, you are contradicting your own message which will only confuse your spouse. Likewise, avoid double messages; let every message be single and clear. *Recognise* that each event can be seen from a different point of view. Do not assume that everyone else sees things as you do; recognise that disagreement can be meaningful but avoid destructive arguments. *Be concerned* more about how your communication has affected the other, rather than getting bitter if you are misunderstood.

Be loving: Stress love above all in your relationship with your partner. Love is not physical attraction. It is not a sentimental wishy-washy affection. Mature love knows how to relate to the needs and interests of others. True love is powerful, sacrificial and giving; it reflects the love of God.

Be spiritual: The spiritual life of the home carries its own authority. Invest yourselves in spiritual values. You can't buy a pound of love or a yard of patience from any supermarket. You can only create such values from within your spiritual selves.

Resolving conflicts

In spite of every effort to have a loving and smooth marital relationship, conflicts can still arise. When they do, one need not be alarmed. Conflicts need not always be destructive or threatening. Conflict has also a bright side to it. It is a sign that the marriage is alive. It can be a means of growth. Couples who learn to argue well are more likely to have a happier marriage than those who repress the differences. However, one need not invite conflicts, and when they arise, they must not be kept unresolved. It helps if the couple agree on certain rules for resolving conflicts.

Separate the person from the problem: Treat one another with respect. Do not abuse. Avoid name calling or character judgement. Understand the other side's perception. Put aside your own feelings and listen to your partner.

Focus on issues, not on positions: Identify the common issue which is the source of conflict. Concentrate on solving the issue rather than on the different positions both of you have taken on the issue. Stick to the point and do not reopen past wounds that have healed. Think of yourselves as partners even when searching for a fair agreement.

Think of various options as a solution to the problem. Let each side make suggestions in a brain-storming session or two. Then evaluate each option.

Have some objective criteria: Before starting the argument, agree on an objective way to reach a solution. For example, if both agree to abide by the results of a coin-toss or a mediator's ruling, accept the outcome according to the criteria, though it may be equally dissatisfying to both of you.

Choose an appropriate time and place: It is never a good idea to argue, for example, if one or both parties have been drinking. It is never a good idea either to argue in front of children.

Keep things in perspective: Remember that you have started an argument, not with a view to breaking away, but to coming closer together. When you are arguing, never forget that you are two people trying to settle into one life.

Forgive and forget: Offer forgiveness to your spouse if you have been hurt; ask for forgiveness if you have caused hurt. And then, get on with it. Grudges are obstacles to a long, loving relationship. Sometimes, compromise may not be possible. If so, accept the fact and get on with your marriage.

HIS WORD COMFORTS

"A man will leave his father and mother and be united to his wife, and they will become one flesh." (Gen 2:24)

The legal union of husband and wife gives them the freedom to depart from their parents. Those couples who ignore this legal element can have still love and sex between them, but they will find no real reason to give themselves to responsible marriage building. On the other hand, couples who are legally married but not united in heart and mind will find their marriage empty. "Marriage is an act of will that sacrifices and involves a mutual gift, which unites the spouses and binds them to their eventual soul with whom they make up a sole family" (Pope John Paul II). Becoming "one flesh" goes beyond sexual union. It means sharing not only bodies and material possessions, but also thinking, feeling, joys, hopes and fears. To achieve such a union will call for a life-long repeated effort. Making a marriage work is in fact like running a farm. You have to start all over again each morning. This is why the critical period in matrimony is perhaps breakfast time.

"Why do you observe the splinter in your brother's eye and never notice the great log in your own? Take the log out of your own eye and then you will see clearly enough to take the splinter out of your brother's eye."

(Mt 7:3-5)

Interpersonal conflicts between spouses often result from abrasive action because of an unforgiving attitude towards faults in another person. We are quick to see faults in others but much slower to see our own. We can bear our own faults, so why not a fault in one's own spouse? Is it not true that each one of us finds in others the very faults others find in us? Our own faults are not minimised by magnifying the faults of others. We easily find fault with others but are quick to defend our own faults, which only proves that we have no intention of quitting them. Be patient with the fault of your spouse, because he or she may have to be patient with yours.

"Where do these wars and battles between yourselves first start? Is it not precisely in the desires fighting inside your own selves? You want something and you lack it; so you kill. You have an ambition that you can't satisfy; so fight to get your way." (Jas 4:1-2)

Faulty communication is said by some to be the most common cause of marital discord. But psychologist Lawrence Crabb, citing the above biblical text, notes that communication problems inevitably result where people pursue self-centred goals. Marriage may be inspired by music, soft words and perfume, but its security lies in the couple's selflessness. To sacrifice one's own self-interest for the sake of the other may be hard, but one has to remember that marriage is an investment that pays you dividends, provided you pay interest. If you entered into marriage for purely selfish motives, then you were blind leading the blind, both falling into matrimony. Those who marry with self-centred goals soon find their home turning out to be a cage, into which they were once desperate to get, but now are equally desperate to get out. Therefore, a successful marriage demands a divorce, yes, a divorce from one's own self-love.

"As much as possible, and to the utmost of your ability, be at peace with everyone." (Rom 12:18)

Every bird of prey wants to consume its booty in tranquillity. Marital peace is not this kind of tranquillity. Peace in the family results from mutual love and mutual respect for each other's individual uniqueness. Many married people think that when they marry they possess their partner much as they possess a fridge or a car. But man and wife don't belong to one another; they have been given to one another. They must be allowed to keep their identity, like the pillars in a temple, where the pillars stand alone, but because of that, they carry the beautiful ceiling.

"They who wait upon the Lord shall renew their strength."
(Is 40:31)

As someone once said, marriage is like a zipper. There are two rows of teeth on a zipper. These teeth fit into one another very neatly. But you need the little zip to draw the teeth together and lock them. The husband and wife need God like a zip, to keep themselves together. Many homes are low in stamina and are fainting because they do not use the spiritual resource which is God. The home needs family religion, not so much as a formality but as a practical everyday response to God. Unless a priority is given to spiritual things, "what God has joined", man will easily put asunder. It is a pity that, because of their concern for success in life, some spouses crowd out God who alone can give success. A home needs God's grace and an absence of God is the corrosion of life. Union with God on a daily basis helps the couple to overcome differences and difficulties. It guides the way towards steady maturity in love. It nurtures the marriage with a consciousness of its sacred destiny and it supports the companionship to ripen in advanced years.

A PRAYER

O God, we were in love and married for life.
But now we are divided and our marriage is
*   breaking;*

we are hurt, wounded, angry and disillusioned;
we no longer find joy in each other and it is
  unbearable.
We realise that our hearts were not
  God-centred;
hence, instead of building our hopes on you,
  our rock,
we tried to build on the smooth sands of selfish
  goals,
which looked good and felt flat, but could not
  stand a storm.
We are sorry; you were never at the centre of
  our lives,
that inner point of sanity; and so, our tempers
  are high.
O Gentle God, we come to you, give our lives
  all to you,
every detail, every barb and every frustration.
Take the scream of anger from the wheels of
  our passions,
that the power of your grace may smooth the
  way we love.
Help us to think before we speak and to
  be quiet,
when we feel that we are going to blaze out.
You alone can refresh our spirits and wash our
  wounds,
for you are a river of hope in the desert of
  despair.
By your grace, may our hurts be healed and
  forgiven.
As the beautiful rose rises from amongst its
  thorns, so,
may our love for each other rise above the storms.